Malcolm X

2014 Treba

Bookmarks
London, Chicago and Melbourne

Malcolm X:
Socialism
and Black
Nationalism

Kevin Ovenden

Malcolm X. Socialism and Black Nationalism
/ *Kevin Ovenden*
Published July 1992
Bookmarks, 265 Seven Sisters Road, London N4 2DE
Bookmarks, PO Box 16085, Chicago, Il. 60616, US
Bookmarks, GPO Box 1473N, Melbourne 3001, Australia
© Kevin Ovenden and Bookmarks
ISBN 0 906224 71 3
Printed by Cox and Wyman Limited, Reading, England

Bookmarks is linked to an international grouping of
socialist organisations:
AUSTRALIA: **International Socialists**,
GPO Box 1473N, Melbourne 3001
BELGIUM: **Socialisme International**,
Rue Lovinfosse 60, 4030 Grevignée
BRITAIN: **Socialist Workers Party**,
PO Box 82, London E3 3LH
CANADA: **International Socialists**,
PO Box 339, Station E, Toronto, Ontario M6H 4E3
DENMARK: **Internationale Socialister**,
Ryesgade 8, 3, 8000 Århus C
FRANCE: **Socialisme International**,
BP 189, 75926 Paris, Cedex 19
GERMANY: **Sozialistische Arbeitersgruppe**,
Wolfsgangstrasse 81, W-6000, Frankfurt 1
GREECE: **Organosi Sosialistiki Epanastasi**,
PO Box 8161, 10010, Omonia, Athens
HOLLAND: **Groep Internationale Socialisten**,
PO Box 9720, 3506 GR Utrecht
IRELAND: **Socialist Workers Movement**,
PO Box 1648, Dublin 8
NORWAY: **International Socialister**,
Postboks 5370, Majorstua 0304, Oslo 3
POLAND: **Solidarnosc Socjalistyczna**,
PO Box 12, 01-900, Warszawa 118
SOUTH AFRICA: **International Socialists of South Africa**,
PO Box 18530, Hillbrow 2038
UNITED STATES: **International Socialist Organisation**,
PO Box 16085, Chicago, Il. 60616

Contents

Introduction / *7*

1. The world of Malcolm X / *11*

2. The life of Malcolm X / *19*

3. The thought of Malcolm X / *36*

4. The legacy of Malcolm X / *51*

5. Socialism or black nationalism / *72*

Notes / *89*

Index / *93*

Acknowledgements
I would like to thank Talat Ahmed, Weyman Bennett, Chris
Harman, Gary MacFarlane, Rahul Patel, John Rees and
Pat Stack for criticism and comments at various stages in
the writing of this book.
Thanks are also due to Duncan Blackie, Ahmed Shawki
and Charlie Kimber for redrafting and editing.
Kevin Ovenden, June 1992

Kevin Ovenden is a member of
the Socialist Workers Party in Britain.

Introduction

MALCOLM X was assassinated on 21 February 1965. He had just risen to speak at the Audubon Ballroom in Harlem, New York, when he was gunned down. We don't know precisely who ordered his killing. We know for sure that the entire establishment breathed a sigh of relief at his death.

A British MP, referred to Malcolm as 'North America's leading exponent of apartheid.' The London **Times** called him a 'black extremist' who advocated the 'destruction of the whites.' The following editorial appeared in the **New York Times** the day after his murder:

> Malcolm X had all the ingredients for leadership, but his ruthless and fanatical belief in violence not only set him apart from the responsible leaders of the civil rights movement and the overwhelming majority of Negroes, it also marked him out for notoriety and a violent end...
> Malcolm X's life was strangely and pitifully twisted. But this was because he did not seek to fit into the society or into the life of his own people...
> The world he saw through those horn-rimmed glasses of his was distorted and dark. But he made it darker still with his exultation of fanaticism. Yesterday someone came out of the darkness that he spawned and killed him.[1]

This was the culmination of a sustained campaign of media vilification waged against Malcolm since he had come to national prominence in 1959.

Such sentiments were not confined to white defenders of the system. Black syndicated columnist Carl T Rowan saw Malcolm as 'an ex-convict, ex-dope peddler, who became a racial fanatic ... A black who preached segregation and race hatred.' Civil rights leader Bayard Rustin called on people to bury Malcolm's ideas with him:

> Now that he is dead we should resist the temptation to idealise Malcolm X, to elevate charisma to greatness. Malcolm is not a hero of the movement, he is a tragic victim of the ghetto.[2]

Walter C Carrington of the National Association for the Advancement of Colored People described Malcolm's politics as the 'best thing that happened to the KKK [Ku Klux Klan] since the invention of the bedsheet.' Ralph Bunche said that he was 'mentally depraved.'

Yet, despite such abuse, Malcolm X remains today—along with Martin Luther King—the best known figure of the black movement of the 1960s. He has become a symbol of resistance to racism. His image is everywhere, from T-shirts to the ubiquitous poster of Malcolm standing, gun in hand, by a window above his slogan, 'By any means necessary'.

The recognition of Malcolm's significance could even be detected back in 1965 under the welter of abuse designed to bury his memory. Nine months after Malcolm's assassination the editors of the **New York Times** printed a review of his posthumously published **Autobiography**. After describing the then conventional view of Malcolm as a violent, racist fanatic the reviewer goes on:

> There is, however, another view of Malcolm X—one that is increasingly prevalent among civil rights advocates—that with his death American Negroes lost their most able, articulate and compelling spokesman.[3]

The liberal magazine, **The Nation**, which in March had described Malcolm as a leader of 'the lunatic fringe' declared in another November review of the **Autobiography**: 'This is the story of a man struck down on his way to becoming a revolutionary and a liberator of his people.'[4]

Today the enormous popular respect for Malcolm's legacy is too tempting to be missed out on by many black leaders who either had opposed him while he lived or would have if they had been around.

Jesse Jackson was one of the keynote speakers at a meeting held in 1990 to commemorate the 25th anniversary of Malcolm's death. In 1984 and 1988 Jackson sought the presidential nomination of the Democratic Party and he has tied his political fortunes to that party. Malcolm described both the Democrats and the Republicans as 'vultures sucking on our blood' and argued against having anything to do with either of them. In 1963 he said: 'Any Negro who casts a vote for the Democratic or Republican parties is a traitor to his own race.'

Louis Farrakhan of the Nation of Islam also claims Malcolm X's mantle. Yet Farrakhan wrote only two months before Malcolm's murder:

> Only those who wish to be led to hell or to their doom will follow Malcolm. The die is set, and Malcolm shall not escape ... Such a man as Malcolm is worthy of death...[5]

Malcolm's legacy has therefore been picked over and torn apart by those whose politics he opposed during his life. What is left in the hands of people like Jackson or Farrakhan is distorted, caricatured and sanitised. The Russian revolutionary Lenin once noted this as a common fate:

> During the lifetime of great revolutionaries, the oppressing classes constantly hounded them, received their theories with the most savage malice, the most furious hatred and the most unscrupulous campaigns of lies and slander. After their death, attempts are made to convert them into harmless icons, to canonise them... while at the same time robbing the revolutionary theory of its substance, blunting its revolutionary edge and vulgarising it.[6]

When the black mayor of New York, David Dinkins, went to speak to black youth who were rioting in the Crown Heights area in 1991 he was chased away. Only hours earlier he had ordered the cops to go in. He returned three days later replete with Malcolm X baseball cap to ensure he got a hearing.

These cynical manoeuvres have only added to the confusion that already surrounds what Malcolm X stood for. The legacy appears more complex still as there are many competing claims on Malcolm's political tradition.

Finally, there is an extra twist as Malcolm's own ideas changed dramatically, particularly in the last 11 months of his life, as he struggled to find a strategy for black liberation in the US and internationally.

The aims of this short book are three fold. The first is to examine the life and times of Malcolm X to see how he and tens of thousands of others like him were shaped by the society they found themselves in and by their attempts to build a movement that could smash the racism, oppression and exploitation built into US society.

I also aim to critically assess Malcolm's political ideas and those of the black movement which exploded in the wake of his death. At its peak this movement mobilised tens of thousands and had the support of hundreds of thousands more. Along with the fight against the war in Vietnam, the struggle against racism threw the entire US ruling class into disarray, shaking the very foundations of the richest and most powerful society on Earth.

Yet by the early 1970s this movement had gone. Despite losing the war in Vietnam and facing open rebellion at home, the US ruling class held on to power. Today, while a new layer of middle class blacks has emerged, the bulk of blacks in the US are no better off than they were 30 years ago.

Malcolm had predicted at the time of his death that the riots then exploding across the US would continue and deepen. The uprising which rocked Los Angeles in 1992 is confirmation, in Malcolm's words, that 'all the evils of a bankrupt system still exist.'[7]

How could such a movement, which looked so promising in the late 1960s, be defeated and give way to the despair which has characterised the past decade?

Finally, this book seeks to find a way forward for the struggle against racism today, by drawing on the experience of generations of socialists and anti racists in both the US and Britain.

Malcolm X was an uncompromising opponent of the system which breeds racism, imperialist domination and exploitation. In the course of this battle he struggled, in often contradictory and confused ways, to develop new ideas and strategies to take account of the turbulent situation. We owe it to him to look hard at the strengths and weaknesses of what he had to say and measure it against experience. We also owe it to ourselves—the issues we face are too important for us to fall back on rhetoric.

The world of
Malcolm X

MALCOLM X was born Malcolm Little on 19 May 1925 in Omaha, Nebraska. His early life was a microcosm of the fate of blacks in the United States—dominated by violence and racism. He was to later note in his **Autobiography** that his father had, 'seen four of his six brothers die by violence, three of them killed by white men, including one by lynching.'[1]

In the late 1920s the Little family moved to Lansing, Michigan. In 1929 their house was fire bombed by racists, the earliest event Malcolm could recall:

> My mother, with the baby in her arms, just made it into the yard before the house crashed in, showering sparks. I remember we were outside in the night in our underwear, crying and yelling our heads off. The white police and firemen came and stood around watching as the house burned down to the ground.[2]

If the police did nothing to put out the fire they were certainly not going to investigate the outrage. They promptly arrested Malcolm's father, Earl Little, on suspicion of arson and for carrying a revolver without a permit.

Such racist violence was happening across the United States. Racism was and is a central feature of American society. Blacks had come to America as slaves. Millions were shipped from Africa to work the plantations of the South. Millions died in transit, millions more perished in the fields. This ultimate barbarity was inflicted on black people at the same time as their European owners were declaring all people to be 'free and equal'. The capitalists who were responsible for the slave trade therefore got out of this contradiction by declaring that, yes 'all men are equals' but that black men were not 'men', they were sub human.

That's how Thomas Jefferson, a slave owner, could sign the Declaration of Independence which begins: 'We hold these truths to be self evident ... that all men were created equal.' Modern racism was born, a product of a rapacious capitalist system, and invaluable in justifying it.

The Civil War of 1861-5 resulted in the abolition of slavery in the South. Racism, however, remained. The short-lived 'Reconstruction' of the South along northern lines failed. The ruling class in the South fought against the advancement of blacks which would threaten their position. Above all, they sought to head off any unity between black and white share-croppers.

Similarly, the capitalists in the North fostered racism in the industrial centres to systematically divide and weaken working class organisation, and preserve their power over all workers, both black and white. As black abolitionist Frederick Douglass put it: 'They divided both to conquer each'.

The situation that developed at the end of the nineteenth century characterised America through to the mid 1960s. In the southern states a system of virtual apartheid existed. The Jim Crow laws—established in the 1870s—segregated schools, transport, housing, wash rooms, restaurants, in fact almost all areas of life. Blacks were either denied the vote through property qualifications, poll taxes and literacy tests or intimidated out of registering.

All institutions—from the police and courts to state govern-ments—were thoroughly racist and combined together to hold blacks 'in their place'. Just to make sure no one resisted or fought back, the Ku Klux Klan would terrorise black neighbourhoods with lynchings and burnings. The Klan had been formed as a white supremacist vigilante group at the end of the Civil War but scarcely existed by the beginning of this century. Its relaunch was trumpeted by America's first full length film, **The Birth of a Nation**, released in 1915.

In the North there were no Jim Crow laws, but there was segregation. Black people were concentrated in ghettoes like New York's Harlem or the South Side of Chicago. Racism flourished and dominated the lives of those such as Malcolm and his family.

Even in these grim times, however, there were organisations which attempted to resist such racism. Malcolm's father and his mother, Louise, both belonged to one, a factor which made the family a special target for racist attack.

Marcus Garvey

EARL AND Louise Little were followers of Marcus Garvey, who led the largest black movement to date, the Universal Negro Improvement Association (UNIA). Garvey founded it in Jamaica in 1914 with the slogan 'One god, one aim, one destiny.' He observed that although there was a British government, a French government and an American government, nowhere in the world was there a black government.

In 1916 he moved to Harlem and set up a branch of the UNIA. By the end of that year he had scarcely 100 supporters. At that time he pursued a strategy of accommodation to racism and looked to Britain to secure an independent black state. He was attracted to the ideas of Booker T Washington, who had encouraged blacks to accommodate to the rise of Jim Crow in the South and argued against the need to fight for political rights, reasoning that 'self help' was the key to black progress.

Blacks were drawn into the workforce during the First World War, with the number of black industrial workers doubling. In 1919 these people expected progress, the press dubbed them the 'New Negro'. This was also the year of a huge strike wave in which a fifth of all workers took part. The bosses tried to divert the rising tide of militancy by playing the race card. They encouraged white workers to blame the newly industrialised blacks for unemployment. They brought in black workers from the South to break strikes by northern whites. The bosses' job was made easier by the refusal of the main unions grouped in the American Federation of Labour to organise blacks and by the way in which the AFL led many strikes to defeat and demoralisation. The result was 26 race riots in the summer of 1919. Unlike in previous pogroms, blacks, uplifted by the new militancy, fought back.

This militancy fuelled the growth of Garvey's UNIA, which was estimated to have 700 branches in 1920 with 350,000 members in New York alone. Garvey had swung left. In 1919 he called for blacks to 'have a white lynched for every Negro who was lynched'. In addition to the ideas of black self help and building black capitalism, Garvey started to argue for racial separation and for blacks to return 'back to Africa'.

He set up the 'Black Star Line' in 1919 to help organise the exodus to Liberia. Very few in fact went. Russian revolutionary Leon Trotsky was later to write:

> They [black Americans] did not want to actually go to Africa. It was the expression of a mystic desire for a home in which they would be free from the domination of whites.[3]

The impact of slogans like 'back to Africa' and 'up you mighty race' boosted black self esteem and gave a sense of black pride in a dehumanising society. But although Garvey could express the desire for change, he could not offer any means of achieving it. As the radicalisation of the early 1920s receded, the UNIA lost its following. As it did so the movement became more inward looking and the positive elements of black pride and resistance gave way to reactionary ones of racial purity.

Opposing mixed marriages, Garvey declared they would,

> lead to the moral destruction of both races, and the promotion of a hybrid caste that will have no social standing or moral background.[4]

As he bitterly attacked socialists, he began to identify with white supremacists, saying at least they understood the need for racial purity. In 1922 he met the Ku Klux Klan's deputy leader in Atlanta and commented:

> I regard the Klan, the Anglo Saxon Clubs and White American societies, as far better friends of the race than all other groups of hypocritical whites put together.[5]

Even worse was to come in the 1930s. When Mussolini's troops invaded Abyssinia he proclaimed, 'We were the first Fascists ... Mussolini copied Fascism from me'.[6]

As Garvey's movement came to such a tragic dead end, the Little family was shattered once more by racist violence. Earl Little died in September 1931. He was found on a Lansing street with his left arm gashed and his left leg almost severed. Controversy surrounds the cause of these injuries but there's no reason to doubt Malcolm's own assessment that his father was murdered by racists. Malcolm's mother, Louise, was left to bring up eight children in depression-hit America. The strain was too much for her. On 9 January 1939 she was declared insane and committed to Kalamazoo asylum.

Malcolm, already expelled from one junior high school, managed to scrape through his second. He moved to Boston to stay with his half sister Ella and got a job as a shoe shiner at the Roseland State Ballroom. For the next six years Malcolm moved from one dead end job to another—living in Boston, Lansing, New Haven and Flint—before ending up in New York. There he became a hustler playing the numbers, dealing drugs and pimping.

In moving from the rural Midwest to New York Malcolm was making the same journey as hundreds of thousands of black Americans. In the early years of this century America's black population was overwhelmingly rural. But as a result of the demand for labour during the First World War the number of black industrial workers grew from 551,825 to 910,181. Detroit's black population grew from 5,741 in 1910 to 40,000 in 1920 and 125,000 in 1930. The recovery from the Great Depression in the mid 1930s drew more blacks into the cities. This accelerated with increased economic growth during the Second World War and throughout the 30 years of sustained boom which followed it. Cities swelled North and South, the countryside was depleted.

Although drawn into the industrial working class, black workers found themselves in the worst jobs, crammed into ghettoes, and with inferior segregated education. Nor did they all find employment. Many like Malcolm found themselves pushed to the margins of society, left with no other source of income than petty crime. Even during the long post war boom one economist reported in 1967 that 1953 was,

> the last year in which blacks enjoyed relatively good times. During 1954 black unemployment went from 4.1 percent to 8.9 percent, double the rate for white workers.[7]

In 1960 44 percent of black people were living in housing unfit for habitation.

Nevertheless, these demographic changes were permanent and tremendously significant in shaping the struggles to come. Black workers in the cities, no matter how ghettoised and repressed, were in a better position to fight against the system than poor sharecroppers. The latter, although they did organise, were far less cohesive and thus easy game for the Klansmen or state authorities. City blacks on the other hand had not only become concentrated in places like Washington, the seat of government, but also worked in the auto factories in Detroit, in the steel mills and manufacturing.

As the conditions for a fightback were being created, the reasons for one were not being diminished in the slightest. Malcolm himself was at the sharp end of a system which gave no hope of legal improvement to virtually all blacks. In 1946 he was convicted for burglary, sentenced to eight to ten years hard labour and sent to Charleston prison. A year later he was transferred to Concord Reformatory and then to an experimental penal colony at Norfolk, Massachusetts. It was while there in late 1948 or early 1949 that he converted to the Nation of Islam, having learnt of it from some of his relatives. He also joined the debating club and rapidly became its best orator. The Nation of Islam, and Malcolm with it, were soon to be propelled to prominence as a result of changes taking place in society outside.

Civil rights and social crisis

THE SLOW changes which had taken place in the structure of US society—the northern movement of blacks, their urban-isation and their penetration of the industrial workforce North and South—put increasing pressures on the political set up.

Although there was considerable resistance to change, the needs of American capitalism had changed considerably since the 1920s—both North and South. The massive expansion of US capitalism which followed the Second World War created thousands of new jobs, straining the racist job reservation policies which existed in many industries. The boom also raised the expectations of all workers—black as well as white—as they sought to achieve the conditions promised by the ruling class.

Not that any section of the establishment wanted a change. Since the end of the Civil War the northern ruling class, grouped around the Republican Party had cared little about racism and urban poverty as long as their economy functioned efficiently.

Nor did they care that in the South everything was run by the same establishment who had fought in the Civil War to preserve slavery. The South was run as a one party state by the Democrats—the party supported by the section of the American ruling class who fought longest and hardest to keep blacks under a state of virtual apartheid.

Change, when it came, was not inspired by either the Republicans or Democrats, but by the struggles of southern blacks themselves. The mid 1950s saw the first stirrings of the civil rights movement. After a brief lull in 1958-9 this movement was to explode across the United States.

In 1954 the American Supreme Court had adjudged in the Brown versus Topeka Board of Education case that racially segregated schooling was unconstitutional. The case had been brought by the National Association for the Advancement of Colored People (NAACP), a moderate black organisation founded by WEB DuBois in 1909. There had been little or no campaign, the strategy had been purely legalistic.

The decision was a victory for civil rights but it left a problem. How was desegregation to be forced on the Southern states? It also raised further expectations of desegregation in other areas. But even the token moves towards civil rights had given way to a profoundly conservative consensus among both the political parties. At the same time as the US bosses were trumpeting the post war years as a new dawn of prosperity, advancement for blacks of all classes was blocked by racism. The pressure for change grew.

It was in this atmosphere that in 1955 Rosa Parks, a member of the NAACP, refused to give up her seat to a white woman on a bus in Montgomery, Alabama. She was arrested. Normally that would have been the end of the matter but Rosa Parks rang some friends, many of whom were activists in the NAACP or in the unions, and began to organise.

The Montgomery bus boycott was born. It lasted a year with almost the entire black population refusing to use the buses. The organisers faced intimidation from racist thugs, houses were firebombed, activists beaten up and even killed. Despite all this, the boycotters won. Montgomery's buses were desegregated. The Montgomery events received massive attention and victory inspired civil rights activists everywhere. It also propelled one of the organisers, Martin Luther King, to nationwide prominence.

The nature of racism in the South shaped the leadership and

strategy of this movement. The overwhelming majority of southern blacks were workers or poor farmers, but there was also a tiny black middle class. The Jim Crow laws affected all blacks. Middle class clergymen and professionals had to use segregated wash rooms just like black sharecroppers.

The leadership of the civil rights movement came from this fragile, urban black middle class. Martin Luther King was a Baptist minister. That the movement in its early phase should have a semi religious ideology should come as no surprise. For decades the Baptist church had been one of the few places where Blacks could congregate in large numbers.

These were the first stirrings of a movement that was to spread across the whole of the United States. Slowly, timidly at first, the civil rights movement began to force the pace of change. In doing so they came up against the southern white supremacists and rankled those in the federal government who wanted to do as little as possible.

They also ignited a fire which would spread beyond the question of legal rights, to the economic and political issues which affected every black in the US and which the ruling class could not afford to concede. Malcolm X was to step to prominence as this movement surged forward.

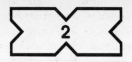

The life of
Malcolm X

The Nation of Islam

MALCOLM SPENT 14 years in the Nation of Islam or the 'Black Muslims' as they were also known. He came to national prominence as its most talented spokesperson and then its 'National Minister' in 1963. During this time the membership of the Nation of Islam mushroomed to over 100,000. What kind of organisation was it, and why did it attract so many people like Malcolm in the 1950s and early 1960s?

The Black Muslims were founded by a Middle Eastern immigrant, Wallace D Fard, in 1930. When he disappeared in 1934 the leadership passed to Elijah Poole who took the name Elijah Muhammad, declared himself 'Allah's Prophet' and ran the organisation until his death in 1975. On joining the Black Muslims, converts would replace their surname by 'X', to signify the unknown African name taken from them by the slave owners.

The formal ideas of the Nation of Islam could best be described as eccentric, although no more so than Christianity in all its variants. Fard maintained that black people in the US were descended from black inhabitants of Mecca. The origins of the white race lay in a bizarre genetic experiment conducted by a warped genetic engineer, Yacub, 6,000 years ago. Allah had decreed that the white race would rule the earth for six millennia and then power would pass over to black people. More accurately, it would pass to those blacks who truly followed Allah—the Nation of Islam. The 6,000 year reign of whites was coming to an end and therefore the salvation for blacks lay in total separation from 'white society', which was doomed to destruction. This could only be achieved through the Nation of Islam.

This inversion of racist pseudo-science, which had claimed

blacks to be 'sub human', undoubtedly appealed to victims of racism. But what really captured people's imagination was the Nation of Islam's rejection of 'white society' and its affirmation of black history and culture. The Black Muslims, and especially Malcolm, gained a reputation for saying what other black leaders did not dare voice. As one commentator put it 'They could have called themselves Black Christians, Black Hindus, or Black Buddhists,' it was the denunciation of the system that won support.

The Nation of Islam also aimed to create a certain sense of black pride. This was obviously present in the religious ideas, but also assumed a particular form in the political and economic outlook of the group and its supporters.

One of the central strategies was the development of black businesses—a strategy which had been present in the ideas of both Marcus Garvey and Booker T Washington. The idea that blacks suffered because they had been cut out of the benefits which capitalism should bestow could have a real appeal under the conditions in the US.

The number of black owned businesses had reached a peak of 70,000 in 1929. The explosive growth of the ghettoes had produced a rash of small businessmen and shopkeepers. They constituted the black middle class right up to the late 1960s. These businesses were orientated on the ghettoes and therefore hemmed in by deprivation and racism. In a certain sense the Nation of Islam echoed the frustrations of that layer of blacks whose path to capitalist success was blocked by racism.

The Black Muslims urged complete economic separation from whites. At the time the majority of blacks worked in white owned businesses. The Muslims argued for blacks to 'buy black'. They also set up dozens of black owned businesses. The aim was clear:

> Everywhere, the Negro is exploited by the white man; now, the black man must learn to protect his own, using the white man's techniques.[1]

Capitalism was on offer, which may have suited the needs of a small section of the black population, but could not solve the problems of the majority. Any growth in black owned business in the ghetto could only benefit a tiny elite and would require the exploitation of black workers, albeit by black bosses. WEB DuBois, an advocate of black capitalism in the 1920s, bemoaned this fact in 1943 when he called on black businesses 'to seek the general economic improvement of all blacks, rather than simply the accumulation of capital at grossly high profit margins.' He was calling on capitalism not to seek a profit, in other words not to be capitalism at all. It could never be.

The black middle class had a wider frustration. Whatever successes they might have in building up some business within the ghettoes, they were totally cut out of the real power houses of the economy. The wealth of the giant corporations was concentrated in the hands of a tiny elite of interconnected families who ran companies such as Ford or General Motors. All blacks and the overwhelming majority of whites were excluded from such wealth. The idea of a parallel black capitalism that could rival the combined might of the US bosses was and is completely unrealistic. The solution therefore offered by Elijah Muhammad was a version of Marcus Garvey's 'back to Africa' call. He wanted a separate black state which could secede from the US. However, the vast majority of blacks were by the 1950s dispersed into concentrations in the cities. What would constitute a black state now? Furthermore, Elijah Muhammad gave no clues as to how the areas with large black populations—including Boston, Chicago, New York and Washington—could be wrenched away from the world's most powerful ruling class.

Growth

THE NATION of Islam expanded from Chicago to build temples in most major cities. In 1952 Elijah Muhammad's entire Detroit congregation could be transported in ten cars; by the early 1960s the Nation of Islam had 100,000 members.

The civil rights movement flared across the South, but it was some years before resistance was seen in the North. As a result, northern blacks felt both the elation of the fight against Jim Crow and frustration at their own rotten situation. By the late 1950s the gap between median black earnings and median white earnings had ceased to narrow. Nevertheless, expectations of improvement continued. There was a growing mood of defiance and people were looking for something to join to express that.

The Nation of Islam capitalised on this mood as it savaged civil rights leaders like Martin Luther King and the NAACP for abstaining from organising in the North.

The Nation of Islam was helped in becoming a rallying point for northern discontent by the lack of any alternative. By 1956 it was virtually the only organisation which could echo the new radicalism. The left had been obliterated by attacks and blunders. The Cold War and McCarthyite purges of the 1950s took a heavy toll on the left. Communists were driven from their jobs and in 1952 11 Communist Party-led unions were expelled from the Congress of Industrial Organisations union federation.

The Communist Party also created its own difficulties by attempting to hitch itself to the Democratic Party. It was pulled to the Democratic Party argument that racism was solely a matter of Jim Crow laws and was therefore confined to the South. The absence of such laws in the North, it claimed, was proof that successful, advanced capitalism would bring liberal benefits to everyone, all that was needed was to overturn the 'anomaly' of the South.

Of course the Democratic Party did not reciprocate the approaches of the Communist Party and its leaders were savage anti Communists. But the important thing was that the Communist Party at this time did not see anything inherently racist about capitalism. The same 'liberal capitalists' it hoped would liberate the South presided over the slums, poverty, and racist police of the North. Such politics offered little to the ghetto dwellers of Watts, Harlem, and Detroit. In addition, the tiny forces of revolutionary socialism were, like their international counterparts, peripheral to the working class movement and riven by splits. The field was therefore left open to the Nation of Islam.

The organisation had a further feature which both made it initially attractive, and created the seeds of its own eventual decline. The Nation of Islam had a policy of extreme abstention from politics. In one sense this was very healthy; in that it refused to endorse either of the official political parties, the Republicans or the Democrats. Both these parties attempted to garner the support of black voters, neither offered anything to solve the problems they faced in terms of police brutality and discrimination over jobs and housing.

However, the Nation's abstention from politics went further than this. It had a strict 'non engagement policy'. This meant not organising alongside non Muslims. Not only did this write off all whites; it excluded most blacks as well. While civil rights activists demonstrated for the desegregation of Little Rock High School in 1957—where the National Guard was called in—the Nation of Islam's leaders could denounce the liberalism of the movement's leaders and their failure to challenge racism in the North. At the same time they did not themselves focus and lead the anger. By the 1960s the Black Muslims were getting the reputation of 'talking tough and doing nothing'.

Malcolm, separatism and the Nation of Islam

MALCOLM WAS the Nation of Islam's best know spokesperson by the late 1950s. The Nation of Islam, and Malcolm in particular, were thrust to national attention in 1959 with a TV documentary by Louis Lomax called 'The Hate That Hate Produced'. Malcolm had said:

> When someone sticks a knife into my back nine inches and then pulls it out six inches they haven't done me any favour. They should not have stabbed me in the first place... During slavery they inflicted the most extreme form of brutality against us to break our spirit, to break our will... after they did all of this to us for 310 years, then they come up with some so-called Emancipation Proclamation... And today the white man actually runs around here thinking he is doing black people a favour.[2]

Lomax described the result:

> within a fortnight every major magazine and news media was carrying long stories about the Black Muslims and particularly about Malcolm. Within a month Malcolm had received invitations to speak from every major university on the East Coast.[3]

What these audiences heard scandalised the American establishment. Malcolm was immediately accused of being a 'black supremacist', a 'racist in reverse' every bit as evil as the white supremacists who had organised the 'White Citizens Councils' as a response to the demands for civil rights. These attacks came, predictably enough, from those hostile to any progress over civil rights but also from leading figures in the civil rights movement as well.

The allegation of 'reverse racism' has always been used against anti racists in an attempt to contain their influence and to roll back anti racist victories. It has been used as an attack on positive discrimination, or affirmative action.

To talk of 'reverse racism' is to miss the point about what racism is. Racism is an ideology that has grown up with and supported the development of capitalism in the US and elsewhere. It is based on the notion of some people being 'inferior' to others. Every racist notion therefore works to support the existing set up, to perpetuate divisions and to reinforce the idea that some people are superior to others on the basis of the colour of their skin.

The arguments of those who react against racism by stressing the need for separate black development are not at all of the same nature. They are a reaction to racism and the existing set up. While separatist ideas cannot in the end overthrow the system that gives rise to racism, they can represent a challenge to it.

The arguments against the allegations of 'reverse racism' were put by the Russian revolutionary Lenin in the first two decades of this century when he looked at the question of nationalism. Writing at a time when the major European powers possessed colonies around the globe, Lenin argued forcibly against the equation of the nationalism of these dominant powers with the nationalism to be found among the nations they oppressed. Nationalism in the oppressor nations bolstered the carve up of the world between the great powers. Support for British nationalism meant support for the occupation of Ireland and the plundering of India. It was entirely reactionary. By contrast, Irish nationalism, or the movement for Indian independence, had, at least in part, a progressive character. They cut against the imperialist carve up of the world. They captured, in however confused a form, a genuine urge for democracy and justice. More to the point, they were a product of imperialist oppression, not the cause of it.

Black separatism and racism are not the same thing. Black

separatism is a response to racism and an attempt to resist it. Nevertheless it is a confused response and one that cannot bring liberation.

Malcolm X was committed to separatism until 1963. We will see later how he broke from the Nation of Islam and how his ideas about separatism and organisation evolved. For now, however, let us look at how Malcolm and the Nation of Islam were affected by the development of the civil rights movement.

The growth of the civil rights movement

THE KEY principle of the southern civil rights movement which had grown under the leadership of Martin Luther King was that of non violent mass civil disobedience. This involved mobilising people in 'peaceful' confrontation with the authorities. 'Peaceful' is not an entirely appropriate term: the demonstrators were non violent, the authorities and racists were anything but. King told the racists and the establishment:

> We will soon wear you down by our capacity to suffer, and in winning our freedom we will so appeal to your heart and conscience that we will win you in the process.[4]

The aim was simple, to embarrass the federal authorities into action. However, the tactic of non violence and the strategy of pressing for action from Washington were both to be stretched and challenged as the movement progressed.

The civil rights movement became a genuine mass movement in 1960. Its base of activists shifted from clergymen to students and the numbers involved mushroomed. On 1 February of that year four black students from North Carolina Agricultural and Technical College, Izell Blair, Franklin McCain, Joseph McNeil and David Richmond, sat down in the whites-only section of the lunch counter in the Woolworth store in Greensboro. They were not served but refused to move until the store closed. The next day 30 students sat down. On 3 February over 50 blacks and 3 white students joined in.

By April 1960 over 50,000 students, black and white, had been involved in the sit-in movement which had spread across the South. Students were beaten up by white supremacists during the sit-ins. Tens of thousands were radicalised, thousands went on to form the core of a new phase in the civil rights movement.

In April 1960 the Student Nonviolent Coordinating Committee (SNCC) was formed. Although it was initially sponsored by King's moderate Southern Christian Leadership Conference (SCLC), it became increasingly independent of it. Together with the Congress of Racial Equality (CORE), which became reactivated during 1958-60, SNCC went on to organise the 'freedom rides' of 1961.

At the end of 1960 the US Supreme Court outlawed racial segregation on inter state buses and trains in the Boynton versus Virginia case. CORE's national director, James Farmer, SNCC's John Lewis and 11 others, black and white, set off south from Washington in May 1961. The freedom riders were attacked in Rockhill, South Carolina on 9 May. A few days later racist mobs burned the bus in Anniston, Alabama.

There followed in breathtaking succession the movement to desegregate Albany in 1961-2; voter registration drives in the heart of the Jim Crow South in Mississippi; and a renewed focus on desegregating the colleges with James Meredith's attempt to enrol at the University of Mississippi which forced the Kennedy administration to intervene with 320 federal marshals. Significantly, CORE attempted to build in a number of northern cities, organising 'sit outs' where poor blacks would block the pavements to protest at appalling housing conditions in the slums.

The increased intensity of the struggle began to lead not only to larger numbers of activists but to sharper political debates about the way forward. As with any mass movement in its initial phase, the civil rights movement encompassed a variety of ideas and tendencies. These differences were muted as the movement gathered speed. In 1960 scarcely anyone doubted King's non violent strategy. But as the confrontations grew bigger, in particular with the federal government under Kennedy, the tendencies started to diverge.

To some extent the strategy of embarrassing the federal authorities had worked. Worried about its international image, the US ruling class under Kennedy and Johnson eventually passed civil rights legislation and intervened in the South. But by the early 1960s the idea that it would be possible to get rid of segregation in the South, let alone racism in the North, by relying on the Democrats was increasingly seen as an illusion.

The Kennedys—John and his Attorney General brother, Bobby—had demanded an enormous price in return for limited support for the civil rights movement. As one historian put it:

> Following the freedom rides, the Kennedy administration made attempts to funnel activists of the civil rights organisations into voter registration activities instead of disruptive movements. Indeed, the Kennedy administration was adamant in opposing widescale civil disobedience. President Kennedy thought low key voting activities would result in peaceful change and provide additional votes for the Democratic Party.[5]

According to James Farmer of CORE, Bobby Kennedy called in CORE and SNCC leaders and told them:

> Why don't you guys cut all that shit, freedom riding and sitting in shit, and concentrate on voter registration. If you do that, I'll get you tax-free status.[6]

By 1963 President John Kennedy and Vice President Lyndon B Johnson had gutted the 1960 civil rights legislation of any effective clauses as it passed through Congress, with the result that it was 'not worth the paper it was written on'. Kennedy was actually to the right of former Republican Vice President Richard Nixon over the issue. Kennedy and Johnson looked to the endorsement of the powerful 'Dixiecrat' section of the party: the segregationists who ran the South.

The Dixiecrats had threatened 'massive resistance' to the implementation of desegregation. But the Democrats also wanted to win the allegiance of the growing black electorate, so there were formulations about civil rights at the same time as reassurances to the white supremacists that nothing much was to change.

In addition to the link with the Dixiecrats, the Democratic Party was just as committed to running American capitalism as the Republicans. This meant preserving the power of the ruling class at home, and with it the powerlessness of the poor. It meant presiding over massive levels of institutionalised racism, and asserting US power abroad; it was Kennedy who first committed large numbers of troops to Vietnam and it was he who ordered the invasion of Cuba which ended in the Bay of Pigs fiasco. As the movement gained greater militancy in the South, rumblings started in the North and the Democratic Party looked increasingly useless. The new frustration and militancy found a powerful voice in Malcolm X.

By any means necessary

MALCOLM WAS the first to express the new doubts about non violence—for which he drew howls of protest from the establishment. In November 1963 he said:

> Our religion teaches us to be intelligent. Be peaceful, be courteous, obey the law, respect everyone; but if someone puts a hand on you, send him to the cemetery. That's a good religion. In fact that's the old time religion. That's the one Ma and Pa used to talk about: an eye for an eye, a tooth for a tooth, and a head for a head, and a life for a life. That's a good religion and nobody resents that kind of religion being taught but a wolf, who intends to make you his meal... No, preserve your life, it's the best thing you've got. And if you're going to give it up, let it be even-steven.[7]

And he insisted that such uses of violence are completely justified, in contrast to the violence of the racists:

> If we react to white racism with a violent reaction, to me that's not black racism. If you come to me and put a rope around my neck and I hang you for it, to me that's not racism. Yours is the racism, but my reaction has nothing to do with racism.[8]

This was a tremendous step forward. On one level Malcolm was merely making concrete Elijah Muhammad's calls for blacks to 'square up to the white enemy'. But in doing so he was beginning to articulate a practical strategy for confronting racism. It had tremendous appeal for the ghetto poor. It represented the start of his divergence from the Nation of Islam and it struck a cord with a new generation of civil rights activists in the South.

Radicalisation in the South, splits in the movement

DEEP DIVISIONS over aims, objectives and class interests had started to emerge in the civil rights movement. Things came to a head with the March on Washington in 1963.

Only weeks before the march Martin Luther King had come under criticism from conservatives in the movement. In April 1963, during the heroic struggle to desegregate Birmingham, Alabama, 'the Johannesburg of the South', eight Birmingham ministers had called on King to take a more legalistic approach and abandon the methods of mass civil disobedience. They were voicing the concerns of a section of the civil rights leadership centred on the NAACP who wanted to rein in the struggle and rely on the Kennedy administration and northern liberals to pass civil rights legislation.

This stemmed from their view of racism as essentially a southern phenomenon, a relic from the nineteenth century, rather than an integral part of US capitalism. It also reflected their total commitment to the American political system. Even then, with Jim Crow still in force, the emergent black middle class sought to preserve the integrity of the US government even if it meant slower progress towards civil rights.

King responded with his famous 'Letter from Birmingham Jail':

> The Negro's greatest stumbling block in the stride toward freedom is not the...Ku Klux Klanner, but the white moderate who is more devoted to 'order' than to justice...who constantly says 'I agree with you in the goal you seek, but I can't agree with your methods of direct action'; who paternalistically feels that he can set the timetable for another man's freedom.[9]

Despite the limitations of his politics King was genuinely committed to the movement. As the movement shifted left during the 1960s King was to follow it, while always vacillating between its most radical edge and the conservative establishment.

Forces were developing to the left of King. These were based on SNCC and CORE. SNCC members provided the bulk of full time activists on the ground in the South. All activists faced violence and intimidation. NAACP leader Medgar Evers was killed in Jackson in June 1963. The systematic racist terror forced SNCC members to reconsider the strategy of non violence. Their organisational independence from the moderates in the movement allowed them space to reconsider tactics. Their inspiration came from the unfolding movements for national independence in Africa and elsewhere. As early as 1962 CORE was discussing the ideas of the Nation of Islam and provided platforms for Malcolm X in 1963.

The March on Washington had been opposed by Kennedy and was toned down by the organisers to win his approval. There was to be no civil disobedience and the march's focus was to be support for Kennedy's extremely limited civil rights bill. King delivered his famous 'I have a dream' speech, but failed to talk about the racist terror in the South or the duplicity of the Democrats. SNCC's John Lewis had his speech repressed. He was to have said:

> In good conscience we cannot support the Administration's civil rights bill, for it is too little, and too late. There's not one thing in the bill that will protect our people from police brutality ... What is in the bill that will protect the homeless and starving people of this nation? What is there in this bill to ensure the equality of a maid who earns five dollars a week in the home of a family whose income is 100,000 dollars a year?[10]

The march was 250,000 strong. It was an impressive display of support for desegregation in the South, but it failed to become a springboard for a deepening of the struggle. The more militant activists were angry. Malcolm summed up their mood when he described the March on Washington as a 'one-day integrated picnic'.

Parting of the ways

NOT ONLY did Malcolm begin to influence elements of the civil rights movement, the struggle in turn affected him. Although formally committed to Elijah Muhammad's ideas, he was spending more time with non Muslims. He took an increasing interest in the civil rights struggle. In short, he became more political. This created tensions between him and Elijah Muhammad which were to lead to him splitting from the Nation of Islam. Malcolm recalled in his **Autobiography** his own frustrations at the non engagement position of the Black Muslims:

> Privately I was convinced that our Nation of Islam could be an even greater force in the American black man's overall struggle—if we engaged in more action.[11]

He sensed that his own misgivings were shared by many ghetto blacks:

> It could be heard increasingly in the Negro communities: 'Those Muslims talk tough, but they never do anything, unless somebody bothers Muslims.' I moved around outsiders more than most other Muslim officials. I felt the very real potentiality that, considering the mercurial moods of the black masses, this labelling of Muslims as 'talk only' could see us, powerful as we were, one day suddenly separated from the Negroes' front-line struggle.[12]

The bankruptcy of the Nation's official position was shown in 1962 when someone did 'bother some Muslims'. On 27 April the Los Angeles police shot seven unarmed Muslims in cold blood and arrested 16 on trumped up charges. Malcolm went to Los Angeles to organise the Nation of Islam's response. He rapidly realised that it would be possible to build a nationwide campaign in defence of the Los Angeles Seven and that such a campaign could involve non Muslims and become a focus for agitation against police violence. His vision of such a campaign broke out of the sectarian straitjacket of Elijah Muhammad. Malcolm declared:

> It was a Muslim Mosque this time; next it will be the Protestant Church; the Catholic Cathedral; the Jewish Synagogue.[13]

He was pulled back by Elijah Muhammad from organising the planned defence campaign. By now the Nation of Islam had a substantial middle class membership whose dues contributed to a large treasury. This, combined with the organisation's sectarianism, reinforced its inactivity, even over attacks on its own members. The gap between rhetoric and action grew and with it the divide between Malcolm and Elijah Muhammad.

In 1962 the Nation of Islam had held a huge meeting to

which the American Nazi Party was invited. Its leader, George Lincoln Rockwell, and some of his goons attended. They were there to discuss partitioning the United States between blacks and whites. The Nation of Islam had reached the Garveyite dead end. Three years later Malcolm, expelled from the Nation of Islam and freed from its discipline, wrote a telegram to Rockwell spelling out what the nature of their next meeting would be:

> This is to warn you that I am no longer held in check from fighting the white supremacists by Elijah Muhammad's Black Muslim movement, and that if your present racist agitation against our people there in Alabama causes physical harm to Reverend King or any other black Americans who are only attempting to enjoy their rights as free human beings, that you and your Ku Klux Klan friends will be met with maximum physical retaliation from those of us who are not handcuffed by the disarming philosophy of non violence, and who believe in asserting our right of self defence—by any means necessary.[14]

Even before his formal break with Elijah Muhammed, Malcolm had publicly expressed his impatience to get involved politically. He told one reporter:

> But I will tell you this. The Messenger has seen God. He was with Allah and was given divine patience with the devil. He is willing to wait for Allah to deal with this devil. Well, sir, the rest of the Black Muslims have not seen God, we don't have this gift of divine patience with the devil. The younger Black Muslims want to see some action.[15]

The chickens come home to roost

MALCOLM WAS asked at a meeting in New York on 1 December 1963 to comment on the assassination of President Kennedy who had been shot nine days previously. Elijah Muhammad had issued strict instructions to all ministers to refrain from making any public comment on the assassination. Across America people were in mourning for the great 'liberal' hope who legend forgets to tell us also put the brakes on the civil rights movement and launched the large-scale US intervention in Vietnam. Elijah

Muhammad was frightened of alienating respectable people. Malcolm wasn't. He gave this opinion of Kennedy's killing:

> The chickens have come home to roost. Being an old farm boy myself, chickens coming home to roost never did make me sad; they've always made me glad.[16]

Given the record of Kennedy and the Democrats, Malcolm was quite right to say this. Elijah Muhammad didn't see it that way. He suspended Malcolm from the Nation of Islam for 90 days so 'Muslims everywhere could disassociate themselves from the blunder'. It soon became clear that the suspension was in fact an expulsion. In March 1964 Malcolm left the Nation of Islam. In an interview with MS Handler in the **New York Times** published on 9 March he mapped out how he saw his future course:

> Good education, housing and jobs are imperatives for Negroes, and I shall support them in their fight to win these objectives, but I shall tell the Negroes that while these are necessary, they cannot solve the main Negro problem.
> I shall also tell them that what has been called the 'Negro revolution' in the United States is a deception practiced upon them, because they have only to examine the failure of this so called revolution to produce any positive results in the past year.
> I shall tell them what a real revolution means—the French Revolution, the American Revolution, Algeria, to name a few. There can be no revolution without bloodshed, and it is nonsense to describe the civil rights movement as a revolution.
> It is going to be different now. I'm going to join in the fight wherever Negroes ask for my help, and I suspect my activities will be on a greater and more intensive scale than in the past.[17]

As Malcolm split to the left of the Nation of Islam, tensions were building in the civil rights movement between those wanting greater activism and those hoping still to hold out for change through the Democratic Party. In 1964 SNCC launched the 'Mississippi Summer Project'. From June to August 1964:

> Over 1,000 volunteers [mainly black and white students] staffed 38 voter registration projects, 23 community centres and 30 Freedom schools with about 3,500 students.[18]

Three students were killed by racists after coming to the aid of a black congregation whose church had been firebombed: Michael Schwerner and Andrew Goodman, two white New York students who had recently arrived in Mississippi, were shot; a local black man, James Chaney, was beaten to death. President Johnson was forced to send the FBI to investigate. The events of that summer propelled leading figures of SNCC further to the left. SNCC leader James Forman explained:

> The Mississippi Summer Project ... confirmed the absolute necessity for armed self defence—a necessity that existed before the project but which became overwhelmingly clear to SNCC people during and after it.[19]

On the other hand, Martin Luther King later that summer declared his willingness to back former segregationist Lyndon B Johnson in the race for the presidency against Barry Goldwater in exchange for support for a civil rights bill. He went so far as to call on activists to call off agitation for desegregation in case it damaged Johnson's chances. Although independent of the Democrats, King had oscillated back towards them and away from the most advanced elements of the movement. Malcolm's attitude to the election was clear:

> If Johnson had been running all by himself, he would not have been acceptable to anyone. The only thing that made him acceptable to the world was that the shrewd capitalists, the shrew imperialists, knew that the only way people would run toward the fox would be if you showed them the wolf. So they created a ghastly alternative. And it had the whole world—including people who call themselves Marxists—hoping that Johnson would beat Goldwater.
> I have to say this: Those who claim to be enemies of the system were on their hands and knees waiting for Johnson to get elected—because he is supposed to be a man of peace. And at that moment he had troops invading the Congo and South Vietnam! He even has troops in areas where other imperialists have already withdrawn. Peace Corps to Nigeria, mercenaries to the Congo![20]

Early in 1965 King made a secret deal with Johnson's Attorney General, Nicholas Katzenbach, that he would not confront Alabama's state troops on a planned march into Selma.

When 3,000 protesters got to Selma Bridge and faced lines of police King, at the head of the march, instructed everyone to turn round and retreat. SNCC organised a march back to Selma and raised the song 'Ain't Gonna Let Nobody Turn Me 'Round'.

Black sociologist Manning Marable sums up what happened:

> For five difficult years, King had been the glue which kept the civil rights united front intact. Leaders to his right— [Andrew] Young, [Philip A] Randolph, [Roy] Wilkins—could accept his activism without personally becoming involved in street demonstrations on a daily basis. He had been a mentor to the left wing... Now the myth was shattered... Robert Allen bitterly denounced King as 'a reluctant accomplice of the white power structure'.[21]

Even though King was to shift to the left, coming out against the Vietnam War and facing massive hostility for doing so in 1966, and then in the last few months of his life organising the poor on a class basis, the movement was radicalising faster than he was.

Another leading figure was more than keeping pace with the radicalisation of the movement: Malcolm X.

He was killed less than a year after his break with the Black Muslims. These last 50 weeks mark an independent phase of his life. Almost half of this time was spent abroad in Africa and the Middle East. Nevertheless from 1964 to February 1965 Malcolm confronted the problems facing the black movement in the US and shifted sharply to the left.

This transition went in fits and starts as Malcolm confronted new problems and engaged with other political ideas. However, two themes came to stand out. The first was that he identified himself as a revolutionary in the broadest sense of the term. He saw oppression and exploitation as fundamental to US society and therefore looked to a solution based on tearing down the structures of oppression rather than attempting to reform them. The nature of such a revolutionary transformation was never fully resolved by Malcolm but he nevertheless looked to some form of revolution as the solution for blacks.

Secondly, in the course of groping towards a solution, he was forced to revise a number of his black nationalist assumptions.

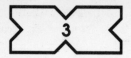

The thought of
Malcolm X

MALCOLM publicly announced his break with the Nation of
Islam on 8 March 1964. Over the next 11 months his political
views changed and developed as he sought to involve himself in
the struggle for black liberation.

In the first few weeks after the break, Malcolm clearly
remained somewhat beholden to Elijah Muhammad. At a press
conference on 12 March he said:

> I still believe that Mr Muhammad's analysis of the problem
> is the most realistic, and that his solution is the best one.
> This means too, that I believe the best solution is complete
> separation, with our people going back home, to our own
> African homeland.[1]

But within weeks Malcolm's organisational break with the
Nation of Islam would also become evident in his own ideas

It is often to the last year of Malcolm's his life that people
look today, either to claim him as an uncritical black separatist,
or to claim that he was becoming a socialist. What were his ideas
in his final hectic year?

Republicans, Democrats and elections

MALCOLM'S DISTRUST of anything to do with establishment
politics in general and the Democratic Party in particular put
him at odds with the dominant strategy of the civil rights movement in the early 1960s, and lay behind the split with the Nation
of Islam. He spelled out his attitude very clearly in December
1964, speaking in reference to the attempt by Fanny Lou

Hammer and the Mississippi Freedom Democratic Party to get black representation to the Democratic Party convention in Atlantic City he said:

> All of these crackers—and that's what they are, crackers—they belong to the Democratic Party. That's the party they belong to—the same one you belong to, the same one you support, the same one you say is going to get you this and get you that ... Lyndon B Johnson is the head of the Cracker Party.[2]

In response to the slogan 'register and vote' Malcolm said:

> What they do with you and me is tell us, 'Register and vote'. Don't register and vote—register! ... you can vote for a dummy, you can vote for a crook, you can vote for another who'd want to exploit you. 'Register' means being in a position to take political action any time, any place and in any manner that would be beneficial to you and me...[3]

However, beyond his hostility to the two established parties, it is not clear that he absolutely ruled out the possibility of elections producing change. He came up with the formulation that freedom would come either through the ballot or the bullet in a famous speech to the Cleveland CORE chapter on 3 April 1964. A week later he pointed to the pivotal role blacks had played in the 1960 presidential election (Kennedy had won by a whisker) and concluded:

> The Negro in this country holds the balance of power... [if he] were given what the Constitution says he is supposed to have, the added power of the Negro in this country would sweep all of the racists and segregationists out of office. It would change the entire political structure of this country. It would wipe out the southern segregationist that now controls America's foreign policy, as well as America's domestic policy.[4]

Malcolm's call 'by any means necessary' meant precisely that if freedom was not going to come through the ballot then it would have to come through the bullet. Towards the end of his life he came to see more clearly that freedom would not come through the ballot. He still did not rule it out as a tactic, but remained unclear as to how such a tactic could fit into a wider revolutionary strategy. Nevertheless, his attitude of contempt towards the Democratic Party and suspicion towards elections is at stark odds with many who want to claim his mantle today.

The role of whites

MALCOLM WAS explicit throughout his time with the Nation of Islam that he saw the struggle against racism as one of all blacks against all whites. For a period after the break he was still dismissive of white anti racists. Asked to pay tribute to a white minister killed during a demonstration to desegregate a school, he said:

> ...what the man did is good. But the day is out when you'll find black people who are going to stand up and applaud the contributions of whites at this late date ... Don't you ever think I would use my energies applauding the sacrifice of an individual white man. No, that sacrifice is too late.[5]

His attitude began to change with the first of two trips he undertook to Mecca and Africa. While on his pilgrimage to Mecca, Malcolm wrote the following in a letter:

> There were tens of thousands of pilgrims from all over the world. They were of all *colours*, from blue-eyed blonds to black-skinned Africans, but were all participating in the same ritual, displaying a spirit of unity and brotherhood that all my experiences in America had led me to believe could never exist between white and non white...
> Throughout my travels in the Muslim world, I have met, talked to, and even eaten with, people who would have been considered 'white' in America, but the religion of Islam in their hearts has removed the 'white' from their minds. They practice sincere and true brotherhood with other people irrespective of colour.[6]

Malcolm converted to orthodox Sunni Islam during this period. In Britain today this is sometimes afforded a central role in the shift of his attitude. The conclusion is drawn that Islam can provide a political theory for achieving a non racist society, as it is a universal religion which knows no bounds of colour.

But on that basis the same case could be made out for

Christianity, which was of course the religion of the slave owners and the European colonisers. Although there may well be a message about the universal brotherhood of man in the Koran, that is no guarantee against racism. Racism is a political force woven into the organisation of capitalist society. It does not come from religious beliefs. Neither is its solution found there. Saudi Arabia, an Islamic country containing the holiest Islamic cities, had a slave market until 1963. As late as 1970 an estimated 500,000 people were still enslaved; many of them were black Africans.

Furthermore Malcolm himself emphasised at this time that he was going to draw a distinction between religion and politics, as he considered it to have been a mistake to confuse the two whilst in the Nation of Islam. The first organisation Malcolm founded was called the Muslim Mosque Inc., but he explained at the time:

> It's true we are Muslims and our religion is Islam, but we don't mix our religion with our politics and our economics and our social and civic activities—not any more. After our religious services are over, then as Muslims we become involved in political action, economic action and social and civic action. We become involved with anybody, anywhere, anytime, and in any manner that's designed to eliminate the evils, the political, economic and social evils that are afflicting the people in our community.[7]

In addition, there are indications that other influences, far removed from religion, also played on Malcolm's ideas at this time. His meeting with the Algerian ambassador to Ghana had an even more dramatic effect in revising his attitudes towards whites. He recalled in an interview in 1965:

> I used to define black nationalism as the idea that the black man should control the economy of his community, the politics of his community, and so forth.
> But when I was in Africa in May, in Ghana, I was speaking with the Algerian ambassador who is extremely militant and is a revolutionary in the truest sense of the word... When I told him my political, social and economic philosophy was black nationalism, he asked me where did that leave him? Because he was white. He was an African, but he was Algerian, and to all appearances a white man. And I said I

define my objective as the victory of black nationalism, where did that leave him? Where does that leave revolutionaries in Morocco, Egypt, Iraq and Mauritania? So he showed me where I was alienating people who were true revolutionaries, dedicated to overthrowing the system of exploitation that exists on this earth by any means necessary. So I had to do a lot of thinking and reappraising of my definition of black nationalism. Can we sum up the solution to the problems confronting our people as black nationalism? And if you noticed, I haven't been using the expression for several months. But I still would be hard pressed to give a specific definition of the overall philosophy which I think is necessary for the liberation of black people in this country.[8]

In the months before his death, Malcolm's changed attitude towards white people became more and more explicit:

I don't speak against the sincere, well meaning, good white people... I have learned that not all white people are racist. I am speaking against... the white racists.

He also said:

I am against every form of racism and segregation, every form of discrimination. I believe in human beings, and that all human beings should be respected as such, regardless of their colour.

Malcolm's reconsideration of his earlier idea that all whites were part of the racist enemy was a huge step forward, but it presented a new problem. If some whites were sincere (he would later say that the sincere ones tended to be socialists) then what was their role in the struggle against racism? Could they be part of a multiracial movement or did blacks have to organise separately?

What kind of unity?

MALCOLM'S VIEWS on the kind of movement it was necessary to build and on the possibility of alliances with 'militant whites' went through a variety of changes. At a press conference to announce the formation of the Muslim Mosque Inc., he declared:

Whites can help us but they can't join us. There can be no black-white unity until there is first some black unity. There can be no workers' solidarity until there is first some racial solidarity. We cannot think of uniting with others, until we have first united among ourselves.[9]

A week later he was to rule out the possibility of any inter racial working class solidarity stating that there had never been 'good relations between working class whites and working class Negroes'[10]; blacks would have to rely on themselves alone to fight racism. The position he held at the end of his life was that unity between the most alienated and 'fed up' sections of whites and blacks was desirable, but difficult to achieve:

You have whites who are fed up, you have blacks who are fed up. The whites who are fed up can't come uptown [to Harlem] too easily because the people uptown are more fed up than anybody else, and they are so fed up it's not so easy to come uptown ...
when the day comes when the whites who are really fed up—and I don't mean these jive whites, who pose as liberals and who are not, but those who are fed up with what is going on—when *they* learn how to establish the proper type of communication with those uptown who are fed up, and they get some coordinated action going. You'll get some changes. And it will take both, it will take everything that you've got, it will take that.[11]

As desirable as such a united outburst of protest from the poor might be, Malcolm continued to argue that this first required some black unity. Both of the organisations he formed, the Muslim Mosque Inc. and then the Organisation of Afro American Unity (OAAU), were dedicated to achieving this.

The slogan of black unity was fantastically appealing to large numbers of blacks. Racism shaped the lives of black Americans. It still does today. Even in Britain, where there is far less segregation than in the US, black people still face day to day harassment from the police and racist thugs; higher unemployment and institutionalised racism in housing, jobs and education; racist immigration controls; and other forms of oppression.

The experience of this kind of racism can lead black people to draw a number of conclusions. The first is that as all blacks suffer racism, then they can all make common cause in overcoming it. The second is that it can appear from experience that all white people, workers as well as bosses, have something at stake in maintaining this state of affairs, or at least think they have. In other words almost all whites will always be at least a bit racist. This perception, which can take hold particularly at times when white workers aren't fighting racism, forms the basis of a black nationalist sentiment.

Organised black nationalists, on the other hand, go beyond this sentiment to draw up a picture of society in which race is the key divide; class is of secondary importance. Quite often this idea has a special appeal to middle class blacks as it cuts out any obligation to fight alongside workers and trade unions in order to tackle racism. Black nationalists would further argue that the struggle must be conducted either by blacks themselves, or 'under the leadership of blacks'. Either way, the central goal is achieving black unity. Although Malcolm rejected the idea of all whites being racist, he continued to argue that black unity and black leadership were essential.

What kind of division?

MALCOLM X recognised that black unity could not just be wished into existence—it had to be fought for. There were many divisions in the movement: the many different strategies which emerged in the civil rights campaign and, of course, there was the public opposition towards Malcolm from the Nation of Islam.

These divisions were not based on personality or temperament, but on different political positions. There was a genuine debate to be had. All great upsurges of anger produce a left and a right wing; people who compromise, people who vacillate, and those who become more militant and intransigent. In part Malcolm recognised the significance of these divisions in founding both the Muslim Mosque Inc. and then the non Muslim OAAU as forums that could involve members of different groups around a common theme.

Malcolm was still formulating his objectives for unity when he was assassinated. We don't know in which direction he might have gone. We can say, however, that the search for black unity would have run up against fundamental problems.

Unity in struggle is always a worthy objective, provided it leads to some action and to a clarification of everyone's ideas. However, there are more fundamental divisions which give rise to differences of politics and strategy than just the individual outlook and experience of different individuals and organisations. There has always been a conservative layer within the black population. Malcolm captured brilliantly the sense of betrayal by those leaders prepared to accommodate to racism. To show the difference between the radicals and the moderates he drew a parallel:

> Just as the slavemaster of that day used Tom, the house Negro, to keep field Negroes in check, the same old slavemaster today has Negroes who are nothing but moderate Uncle Toms, twentieth century Uncle Toms, to keep you and me in check, to keep us under control, keep us passive, and peaceful and non violent. That's Tom making you non violent. It's like when you go to the dentist, and the man's going to take your tooth. You're going to fight him when he starts pulling. So he squirts some stuff in your jaw called novocaine, to make you think they're not doing anything to you. So you sit there and because you've got all that novocaine in your jaw, you suffer—peacefully. Blood running all down your jaw and you don't know what's happening, because someone has taught you to suffer—peacefully.[12]

> If someone came to the house Negro and said 'Let's separate, let's run,' the house Negro would look at that person like they were crazy and tell him, 'Run where? How would I eat if my master didn't feed me? How could I clothe myself if my master wasn't here to give me clothes?'[13]

Such a formulation, however, captures the anger, but not the reason for the sell out. The political divisions between moderate and radical; right and left are not arbitrary. They correspond to the differing interests of blacks in different social positions.

Malcolm saw the division as one between the majority of blacks and those who allowed themselves to be a tool of the 'white establishment'. The cry of 'sell out' can be heard today. It expresses the genuine anger of the impoverished at the lifestyles of the minority of rich blacks, or at the politics of someone like Supreme Court Justice Clarence Thomas who, having benefitted from affirmative action (positive discrimination) measures throughout his life, is committed to overturning them now he has made it.

In Britain a similar attitude is positive when directed at blacks who join the Tory Party, a bastion of the rich and privileged and racist to the core. But it begs the question, what is it that these people are selling out?

The assumption is that at some level or another they have a common interest with the mass of poor working class blacks. They are selling out their race. Such 'betrayal' is often rationalised by saying that they are being 'used by the white power structure'. They are duped by the racists. But the issue is not their own lack of principle, still less their gullibility. They are perfectly conscious of the role they play and fully aware of their own interests.

The problem is that their interests are not the same as those of working class blacks. They stand not as the house Negro to the field Negro, who were both slaves, but, freed from wage slavery, they stand outside of the working class. And, despite their colour, in opposition to workers. Towards the end of his life Malcolm was beginning to grapple with these class divisions.

The inspiration of Africa

MALCOLM AND other black revolutionaries were profoundly affected during the 1960s by the national liberation struggles then unfolding across Africa and other parts of the Third World. On his two travels abroad he met Kwame Nkrumah, president of Ghana, Gamal Abdel Nasser in Egypt, Sekou Toure of Guinea, Milton Obote of Uganda, Nnamdi Azikwe of Nigeria, and Jomo Kenyatta of Kenya. The victory of these independence movements inspired him in the fight for black liberation in the United States.

While on his first visit to Africa he was taken up on his use of the word Negro and informed in Ghana that the word Afro American was more appropriate. On his return he explained:

Negro doesn't tell you anything. I mean nothing, absolutely nothing. What do you identify with?—tell me—nothing. What do you attach to it? Nothing. It's completely in the middle of nowhere. And when you call yourself that, that's where you are—right in the middle of nowhere. It doesn't give you a language, because there is no such thing as a Negro language. It doesn't give you a culture—there is no such thing as a Negro culture, it doesn't exist. The land doesn't exist, the culture doesn't exist, the language doesn't exist and the man doesn't exist. They take you out of your existence by calling you a Negro. And you can walk around in front of them all day long and they act like they don't even see you. Because you made yourself non existent.[14]

The use of the terms Afro American and black grew as the movement grew in the 1960s. It reflected a new found pride among blacks and was a positive development. Malcolm added that it was necessary for blacks to discover black history.

His trips to Africa also inspired him in the direction of what he called 'socialism', on the basis that the new regimes were seen to be fighting against the same enemy as him:

... all of the countries that are emerging today from under the shackles of colonialism are turning toward socialism. I don't think it's an accident. Most of the countries that were colonial powers were capitalist countries, and the last bulwark of capitalism today is America. It's impossible for a white person to believe in capitalism and not believe in racism. You can't have capitalism without racism. And if you find one and you happen to get that person into a conversation and they have a philosophy that makes you sure they don't have this racism in their outlook, usually they're socialists or their political philosophy is socialism.[15]

Some writers claim this as evidence that Malcolm was himself becoming a socialist. True, national liberation had dealt a blow to imperialism. However, the newly independent states took the term socialist as a flag of convenience to describe their alliances with the Stalinist bloc and as a tag for their chosen path of development.

Socialism for many of the newly independent African states meant building up industry through state ownership and competition on the world market. They sought to copy the example of the USSR which, since the 1930s, had marshalled the productive powers of the country under the control of the state and a bureaucratic ruling class.

Malcolm was not alone at the time in calling this socialism, the Black Panthers held similar views and it was the orthodoxy among that part of the left which had abandoned the idea that socialism could only be achieved through the self emancipation of the working class.

Minorities and majorities

THERE HAS always been an obvious problem with the idea that blacks could transform Britain or the US on their own—numbers. There are 32 million black people (those of African descent) in the US; about 13 percent of the population. In Britain the total number of Afro Carribeans and Asians comes to about 3.5 percent of the population. Any black nationalist programme for political change has to confront the fact that blacks are in a clear minority.

Malcolm hoped this difficulty could be overcome by looking at the problem another way on. In April 1964 he reviewed 'two schools of thought' among American blacks. Among one:

> Their thinking is usually domestic, confined to the boundaries of America, and they always look upon themselves as a minority. When they look upon themselves upon the American stage, the American stage is a white stage. So a black man standing on that stage in America automatically is in the minority...
>
> Whereas the other segment or section in America, known as the black nationalists... don't look upon themselves as Americans. They look upon themselves as a part of dark mankind. They see the whole struggle not within the confines of the American stage, but they look upon the struggle on the world stage. And, in the world context they see the dark man outnumbers the white man. On the world stage the white man is just a microscopic minority.[16]

Although he later went on to propose alliances with white militants he nevertheless continued to be scornful of those who said that blacks constituted a minority.

In terms of numbers, the 'world stage' outlook expresses a fundamental truth. It is also true that the struggle against oppression and capitalism is international. Genuine socialists have always insisted upon this. Karl Marx called on the workers of the world to unite. Lenin and Trotsky saw the Russian revolution as the start of a chain of revolutionary upheavals around the world. They rejected the notion of socialism in one country.

Malcolm also argued from the world context against the claim made by the right wing in the civil rights movement that the minority position of blacks in the US meant they had no alternative to an alliance with the Democratic Party. For example, Bayard Rustin attacked Stokely Carmichael's use of the Black Power slogan as simplistic,

> utopian and reactionary—the former for the by now obvious reason that one-tenth of the population cannot accomplish much by itself, the latter because [it] would remove Negroes from the main area of political struggle... [the Democratic Party].[17]

Malcolm was right to reject such demobilising arguments. However, his own outlook was seriously flawed. He never gave a coherent account of how Third World blacks could replace US workers in an alliance powerful enough to break US capitalism.

Of course the struggle against national oppression in Africa had an impact in the West, but what precisely was that impact? How were the struggles in Algeria and Ghana linked with those in Mississippi and New York?

The war in Vietnam provoked huge opposition inside the US after 1968. The struggle of the Vietnamese and the battles of the anti war movement were obviously connected. But it was precisely because the anti war movement became a real, living issue for tens of millions of people in the US that it was effective.

Civil rights had to be fought for and won inside the US itself. There was, needless to say, widespread support for the American black struggle around the world. Such solidarity helped to keep the movement going, convincing Malcolm that he had been successful in 'internationalising our problem' during his second trip to Africa. But the fact remained that the fight against racism and for a better society had to be waged by those Americans who had an interest in it. The mobilisation of hundreds of thousands won the desegregation of the South, not pressure from abroad.

There was another question. With whom should American blacks align themselves in Africa? For most black radicals, including Malcolm, this was hardly an issue. It was almost universally acknowledged that, since these countries had come out of colonial subjugation, everyone, irrespective of class, shared the same anti imperialist revolutionary interests. Many argued that the concept of class was not applicable to these countries, either because African societies could not be understood as class societies or because they were in any case socialist states where class divisions did not exist.

But the attempt by a new ruling class to build up industry and find a way into the world market created large working classes in all these countries with which the rulers were bound to clash. The pressures of the world market and institutions like the IMF and the World Bank meant that these countries suffered recession and crisis even deeper than in the West. The result was not 'shared austerity' among all classes but an intensified class struggle as the rulers of these countries tried to jack up the rate of exploitation and throw the effects of the crisis onto the working class and peasantry.

Many of these developments only became apparent after Malcolm's death. Even so, black nationalists continue to this day to look to various Third World leaders to provide support to the anti racist struggle. Even if they could be relied upon to do this the problem of power remained. How could the African heads of state who together made up the Organisation of African Unity (OAU) force the hand of the American government?

Towards the end of his life Malcolm was working on a plan to get the OAU to indict the American government for crimes against humanity at the United Nations. Even if he could bring this off, the best it could do would be to provide a propaganda victory against the US government. But it could not come off. As the recent history of the UN's role in providing cover for the US war against Iraq shows, the UN is not an arena where small countries can moderate the ambitions and power of larger ones.

It seems incredibly naïve of Malcolm to have pursued the plan of bringing the US before the world court. Of course he saw it as connected with the struggle in the US, he was not abandoning revolutionary agitation for a career in international law. But it was an unnecessary digression which flowed from a false hope that there was some power which could deal with the brutality of American capitalism and which was more effective than the power of the working class in the US itself.

Socialist or nationalist?

THERE CAN be no doubt that Malcolm X stood firmly on the left wing of the movement. His hatred of the system, of both the capitalist parties, his uncompromising challenge to racism and his defence of violence when necessary put him way to the left of many of the other leading figures in the black movement.

However, he was not a socialist, even though we know nothing of what he might have become had he lived. When asked if blacks alone will fight for change in the US, he answered:

> Yes. They'll never do it with working class whites. The history of America is that working class whites have been just as much against not only working class Negroes, but *all* Negroes, period, because all Negroes are working class within the caste system. The richest Negro is treated like a working class Negro. There never has been any good relationship between the working class Negro and the working class whites....there can be no worker solidarity until there's first some black solidarity. We have got to get our problems solved first and then if there's anything left to work on the white man's problems, good, but I think one of the mistakes Negroes make is this worker solidarity thing. There's no such thing—it didn't even work in Russia.[18]

But there is no doubt that Malcolm's views on socialism also changed dramatically. Once, soon after he had broken with the Nation of Islam in March 1964, he answered the question, 'what do you think of socialism?' by saying: 'Why speak of it. If you want someone to drink from a bottle, you never put the skull and crossbones on the label, for [they] won't drink.'

Later that year, however, Malcolm began to speak openly and favourably about socialism, saying white anti racists tended to be socialists. He also located the source of racism at the heart of capitalism:

> It's impossible for a chicken to produce a duck egg—even though they belong to the same family of foul... A chicken just doesn't have it within his system to produce a duck egg. It can't do it. It can only produce according to what that particular system was constructed to produce. The system in this country cannot produce freedom for the Afro

American. It is impossible for this system, this economic system, this political system, this social system, this system, period. It's impossible for this system, as it stands, to produce freedom right now for the black man in this country.[19]

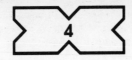

The legacy of
Malcolm X

MALCOLM X was slain barely a year into his most intense period of political transformation. He hardly had time to test his ideas in the cauldron of radicalisation and ghetto risings which marked the late 1960s. Others, however, attempted to take up where he left off. It is to them we must now turn to measure Malcolm's ideas against the test of practice.

Black Power

THE STRUGGLE exploded onto the streets of the North in 1964 when Harlem erupted after the police shot a 15 year old black youth. Police racism was to be the trigger for a wave of ghetto uprisings reaching a peak in 1967-8. The scale was enormous. In February 1965 Malcolm had predicted:

> Well, 1965 will probably be the longest, hottest, bloodiest summer since the beginning of the black revolution, primarily because the same causes that existed in the winter of 1964 still exist in January, in February, of 1965. Now, these are the causes of inferior housing, inferior employment, inferior education. All of the evils of a bankrupt system still exist where black Americans are concerned...[1]

A fairly minor case of police harassment in Los Angeles sparked the Watts uprising in August 1965. At the end of six days of rioting which engulfed 46 square miles of Los Angeles 34 people, 28 of them black, had been killed, over 1,000 injured and 4,000 arrested. Property worth $35 million was destroyed. As whole areas of Los Angeles were gutted, the slogan 'Burn baby, burn!' could be heard above the clamour.[2]

Rioting on a similar scale hit Detroit in 1967. The federal government deployed 15,000 state police and National Guardsmen to suppress the rising. 43 residents were killed (nine white, 34 black), 5,000 people were left homeless.[3]

The sheer scale of the rebellion was daunting. In 1965 there were nine riots, 38 in 1966, 128 in 1967, and 131 in the first six months of 1968. In the eight years from 1964 to 1972 there were 250 deaths, 10,000 serious injuries and 60,000 arrests in the uprisings. The damage to property and the cost of policing amounted to billions of dollars. All this took place as the US state was getting more and more bogged down in the war in Vietnam. After the National Liberation Front's Tet offensive in January 1968 the myth that this was a war that the US couldn't lose was shattered. The war became increasingly unpopular at home.

Against this backdrop, the black movement entered its most radical phase. The slogan which seemed synonymous with it was 'Black Power'.

The slogan was raised by Stokely Carmichael of SNCC on the 'March Against Fear' in Mississippi in 1966. James Meredith, the first black student to attend the University of Mississippi had been shot in June 1966 during a solo march from Memphis to Jackson. Martin Luther King, CORE's Floyd McKissick, and Stokely Carmichael of SNCC pledged to carry on the march. Carmichael wanted the Black Deacons of Defense to provide armed escort for the march, but King ruled that out. After being arrested on the march Carmichael declared:

> This is the twenty-seventh time I have been arrested. I ain't going to jail no more. What we gonna start saying now is 'Black Power'.[4]

Within weeks the slogan was front page news and being debated by activists everywhere. The liberals in the Democratic Party and the conservatives in the civil rights movement united in condemnation. Roy Wilkins fronted the attack at the NAACP July convention:

> No matter how endlessly they try to explain it, the term 'Black Power' means anti white power. It is a reverse Mississippi, reverse Hitler, a reverse Ku Klux Klan... [it is] a quick, uncritical and highly emotional [slogan] that would culminate in 'black death'.[5]

Ironically the Black Power slogan had originally been raised by moderates like Adam Clayton Powell to denote black self advancement. In mid 1966 however it was perceived as a slogan of the radicals, captured the mood of the times and quickly gained popularity.

What was meant by Black Power? To those such as Stokely Carmichael it combined the ideas of black unity and the militancy to be found in Malcolm X's thought. Stokely Carmichael and Charles V Hamilton, in their 1967 book **Black Power**, gave the following definition:

> Black power is a call for black people in this country to unite, and to recognise their heritage, to build a sense of community. It is a call for black people to begin to define their goals, to lead their own organisations and to support those organisations. It is a call to reject the racist institutions and values of this society. The concept rests on a fundamental premise. Before a group can enter open society, it must first close ranks. By this we mean that group solidarity is necessary before a group can operate effectively from a bargaining position of strength in a pluralistic society.[6]

Black Power—a double-edged sword

BOTH CORE and SNCC concluded that Black Power implied the creation of all-black organisations. Within months both CORE and SNCC expelled their white members. Carmichael declared: 'We don't need white liberals... We have to make integration irrelevant.'[7] SNCC had been debating the role of white anti racists for a number of months. Their assessment that white SNCC members had to organise in the white community now became amplified into saying there could be no place for whites in SNCC. The perception was that the 'integrationists'—King, the Southern Christian Leadership Conference and the NAACP —were more conservative because they sought integration with 'white society'. But this was to grossly oversimplify what was happening.

As the struggle intensified and drew victories more painfully from the establishment, the politics of the movement started to polarise. The divergence between the different interests and objectives of those in the movement now began to assert itself. Ideas were being tested in the crucible of action.

SNCC and CORE were not radicalised by the establishment of black-only organisation. SNCC had already become more radical, with many of its members describing themselves as revolutionary whilst it still had white members. Radicalisation came from the movement itself which led tens thousands into confrontation with the American state.

What made the mainstream of the civil rights movement more conservative was that it looked to 'liberal' elements in the ruling class to institute change. It did this because its political outlook was that, provided the appropriate legal measures were in place, blacks could prosper in 1960s America. Capitalism, and with it the American political system, its state and institutions, could be freed of racism. This political outlook in turn reflected the class interests of middle class blacks—essentially advancement within the system. For these reasons the mainstream of the civil rights movement attacked not only SNCC but also King for coming out against the Vietnam war.

Therefore, the common perception of what is represented by the two tendencies in the movement is wrong. The split between integrationists and separatists is not a straight right-left line up, a division between conciliators and the uncompromising. Neither integration nor separation could in themselves be guarantees against compromise. This was certainly to prove the case with Black Power. There was one interpretation of the slogan which the establishment found very easy to swallow. In 1968 right wing Republican Richard Nixon could boast:

> Much of the black militant talk these days is actually far closer to the doctrines of free enterprise than to those of the welfarist thirties... What most of the militants are asking is not separation but to be included in—not as supplicants, but as owners, as entrepreneurs—to have a share of the wealth and a piece of the action. And this is precisely what the federal central target of the new approach ought to be. It ought to be oriented toward more black ownership... black pride, black jobs, black opportunity and yes, Black Power... [8]

In other words Black Power to him meant black capitalism. Nixon was not alone. Black Republican Nathan Wright organised the first Black Power conference in a white owned hotel with a registration fee of $25 (out of the reach of most working class blacks). The majority of the 1,300 who attended were middle class blacks. The Black Power conference of June 1968 was sponsored by the white owned Clairol Company. James Forman describes the disillusionment of black radicals at the time:

> Seeing that they could not destroy the revolutionary thrust of Black Power, the powers of this nation adopted a new tactic—co-optation. It's the good old American way: Whom the gods cannot destroy, they then try to buy off. We first saw the attempt to get Congressman Adam Clayton Powell to hold a Black Power conference in the auditorium of the United States Labor Department. The idea received some serious consideration in the ranks of the militants, but SNCC took the position that to hold such a conference in such a place under such a sponsorship would be to play directly into the hands of our enemies.[9]

The Black Power slogan was unclear. It could be identified with black capitalism, black electoral power, radical nationalism or cultural nationalism.

The SNCC leadership were confused over the way forward. Robert Allen observed that Carmichael,

> attempted to pick up the threads of Malcolm's thought and apply them to this social context. But he was uncertain how to move. He was torn between reformism and revolution.[10]

This wavering over whether the whole system had to be torn up and society founded anew or whether change could come through the existing political structure lay at the root of the confusion. This was doubly dangerous as there were other forces waiting in the wings with their own strategies in the absence of a clear one from the left. The ruling class was anxious to batten on to anything which could co-opt a layer of the movement in order to defuse it. That layer was already in place, in the black middle class leaders of much of the civil rights movement. For them too, it made sense to move towards a position of conciliation with the ruling class rather than struggle. The differing class interests in the movement now made themselves felt.

The most important factor which allowed Nixon and capitalists like the Clairol Company to co-opt Black Power was that they did so with the support of a layer of the black population. Nixon was not practicing an enormous deception on all blacks, cynical as he was. He was relying on the support of the black middle class to sell the whole idea of black capitalism and self advancement. The strategy was effective because it appealed to the interests of the black middle class and found no coherent opposition from a movement which had failed to say that capitalism itself was responsible for racism.

This bad experience for the militants led some of them to form a much more consistent revolutionary black movement at the end of the 1960s.

The Black Panthers

THE BLACK Panther Party for Self Defence was formed in October 1966 in Oakland, California by two students, Huey Newton and Bobby Seale. They took the name and panther symbol from the SNCC-inspired Panther organisation in Lownes county and were immediately influenced by the ideas of Malcolm X. Newton said Malcolm X was the first political person in the US he had identified with.

The idea which they most clearly took up was Malcolm's advocacy of armed self defence. They began to organise among the poor and the working class of Oakland, putting forward a ten point programme of demands which covered democratic, political and economic issues.

It was not so much the content of these demands as the fact that the Panthers were prepared to openly confront the US state in order to win them that pushed them in an explicitly revolutionary direction. In particular point seven, the demand for an end to police brutality brought them full square against the police. They started to 'patrol the pigs' on the streets of East Oakland. This meant following police cars and intervening when the cops harassed blacks on the streets. They also exercised their constitutional right to carry arms and went fully armed with shotguns and rifles. The number of cases of police harassment declined during 1967 in Oakland.

They came to national prominence that year when the California State Legislature set out to change the law to prevent them carrying arms. The image of Huey Newton standing on the steps of the assembly building in Sacremento with a score of other Panthers, dressed in black berets and leather jackets with loaded pump action shot guns, was flashed around the world. By the end of 1968 they had over 5,000 members across America.

Open defiance of the state brought savage repression. Surveillance by the Oakland police was supplemented by the efforts of the FBI. In October 1967 Huey Newton was framed for murder after he and a friend were attacked by a cop in Oakland. The ensuing 'Free Huey' campaign gained an enormous following. Newton was eventually released in 1970.

By then the Panthers had been all but ripped to pieces by repression. Similar treatment was handed out to SNCC and other black radicals. The savagery was not a result of the desire for vengeance. The ruling class was seriously worried by the threat of the radicalised black and anti war movements. In 1971 a secret memo to President Nixon noted that 25 percent of blacks respected the Panthers, including 43 percent of those under 21.

The US state went to enormous lengths to stamp this out. The police killed 28 Panthers in two years. In December 1969, 15 agents from the Cook County Illinois State Attorney's office, armed with machine guns and pistols, raided the local Panther headquarters and murdered two leaders while they slept.

In addition to assassinating leading Panthers, the state framed political activists like Angela Davis, sacked from her job at the University of California by the then governor of that state, Ronald Reagan. George Jackson had been sentenced to 'one-year-to-life' at the age of 18 for stealing $70. He refused to be broken by the prison regime and was placed in solitary confinement for years but continued to write his bestselling **Soledad Brother** and became the Panther's national 'Field Marshall'. He was executed by guards in San Quentin prison in August 1971.

The heroism of thousands of people like Jackson remains an inspiration. State repression was undoubtedly a major factor in the demise of the Panthers and the fragmentation of the left. However, this is not the whole explanation.

The high point of the ghetto uprisings was now passed. By 1969 there was a growing feeling among ordinary blacks that despite the militancy of groups like the Panthers it was not possible to win any fundamental change. Leaders were being shot or going into hiding, simple appeals for more activism or more radical speeches were not drawing in fresh forces. With ups and downs, there had been a sustained revolt throughout the 1960s. There was now a sense of 'war weariness'. The Panthers had to face this reality. But they found it difficult to see a way forward.

The people the Panthers hoped would take up arms, patrol the pigs, and be the 'revolutionary vanguard' were what they termed the 'boys on the block'. These were the unemployed of the ghetto. They were the most downtrodden section of society. Bobby Seale described them as:

> a vast reservoir of revolutionary potential. The lumpen prol-
> etarian brothers on the block, and sisters, and everybody in
> the streets who are trying to make it, are part of this
> reservoir which one day will come forth like a wild, rushing
> stream.[11]

The fact that they were not bound by the discipline of the boss meant they could be the first to explode into activity. But this volatility cut both ways. They could be attracted by the military aspect of the party in a way that employed workers rarely were. But they were also much harder to turn into a cohesive force. They lacked the traditions and discipline that capitalism hammers into those it exploits. Many were tempted back into a lifestyle which provided some kind of living through petty crime. The biggest problem was that they lacked real power. They were not in the position of employed workers who could bring the capitalist system to its knees by withdrawing their labour and crippling its ability to make profits.

These weaknesses of strategy and base meant that when Nixon launched the repression, the Panthers, despite having the sympathy of many blacks, were isolated from the only people capable of withstanding it, the industrial working class.

By the end of 1968 the Panthers' leadership could no longer ignore these questions. They made a turn to 'serious' politics and the Black Panther paper described the party as Marxist-Leninist. Instead of the talk of 'armed self defence', the leaders stressed the slogan 'serve the people', popularised by followers of Mao Ze Dong. This slogan centred on a kind of do-it-yourself social work with local Panther groups supplying breakfasts to, they claimed, 10,000 children in 1969, usually in church premises.

The Panthers also looked for new white allies. In 1968 they

had worked first with the anti war California Peace and Freedom Party, then with the apparently more radical Jerry Rubin and the Yippies. Now, seeking partners to protect them against repression, the Panthers looked to their right. They organised a national conference to which those invited included Democrats and even Republican 'anti fascists'. The failure of this strategy strengthened those who argued for an armed struggle, which proved equally ineffective. The Panthers degenerated into squabbling factions. The magnificent potential had been defeated.

The experience of the Black Panthers is instructive. It was the closest formation to what Malcolm was describing before his death. They were heavily influenced by him and shared many of his strengths and weaknesses. The Panthers were distinguished by their willingness to work alongside radical white groups and their uncompromising revolutionary position. While others were engaged in separatist phrase-mongering, Newton made a point of saying, 'we don't hate whites, we hate oppression'. He recognised the importance of class differences, saying the Black Panther Party would fight racism and capitalism with, 'a solidarity derived from a proletarian internationalism born of socialist ideology.'

The Panthers were not alone in their failure to locate a force which was capable of carrying through a revolution in the US. They shared this with just about every radical at the time.

Ultimately the Panthers were broken apart as they failed to find a real base among workers—black or white. There were other attempts, however, to beat a path to the working class.

'Our thing is DRUM'

IN MID 1968, scarcely a year after the Detroit uprising, the Dodge Revolutionary Union Movement was created by a group of black socialists. It was formed after the victimisation of two workers following a wildcat strike at the Dodge Main Chrysler plant. One of them, General Baker, became a prominent leader. The majority of Detroit's population was black, as were one in four auto workers. General Motors, Ford and Chrysler, dominated the city. Racism was rife in the car plants. At Chrysler's Dodge Main 95 percent of all foremen were white, all the superintendents were white and 90 percent of the skilled craftsmen were white. The majority of the workforce was black. The United Auto Workers had the largest black membership of any union. Yet only one of the 26 people on its executive was black.

DRUM distinguished itself from other radical groups with its insistence on the centrality of the working class to any revolutionary social change. One of its founders, John Watson, outlined DRUM's position: 'Our analysis tells us that the basic power we have lies at the point of production, that the basic power we have is the power of workers.' He put the case for the orientation of revolutionaries on the working class:

> In one factory we have 10,000 people who are faced with the same conditions... When you go out into the community, the interests of the people... are going to be much more dispersed... The kinds of actions which can be taken [in the community] are not as effectively damaging to the ruling class as the kind of actions which can be taken in the plant ... When you close down Hamtrack assembly plant... for a day you can cost Chrysler corporation 1,000 cars.[12]

This is not to say they ignored community based struggle. They attempted to link the community struggles with the power of the auto workers through the DRUM organisation. At one stage they had 700 dues paying members and regularly had 400 at their weekly meetings. The success of DRUM inspired imitation. By 1969 there were Revolutionary Union Movements across Detroit. However, the only other organisation to achieve any success was the Eldon Avenue Revolutionary Union Movement (ELRUM), based at Chrysler's gear and axle plant.

The national umbrella, the League of Revolutionary Black Workers, only lasted two years. From the beginning there were tensions. Watson, Baker and others emphasised a working class orientation and were critical of the nationalists. Other executive members, saw the struggle culminating in the formation of separate white and black states. The nationalists succeeded in blocking attempts to develop a clearer socialist approach. Even those in DRUM who emphasised an orientation on the working class tended to be influenced by black nationalist politics. This was most clearly expressed in DRUM's hostility to the idea of trying to relate to or organise white workers in the plants.

This lack of political clarity became a crucial weakness during periods of calm and lulls in the struggle. Despite setting up a bookshop and organising public meetings they never managed to build an organisation which was capable of relating to different struggles, generalising them and winning a layer of militants to a clear revolutionary understanding of society.

ELRUM refused to give out leaflets to white workers, though many of them were sympathetic to the movement's aims. On one level this was not much of a handicap. Eldon Avenue had a majority black workforce and could be shut if they walked off the job. But if you identified black workers as being in a position to change society *as workers* then that meant looking to the working class as a whole, both black and white, and organising its most militant elements alongside others such as students and the unemployed.

DRUM had no mechanism to consistently influence white workers, many of whom were beginning to become radicalised. They argued that was the job of white radicals. The problem was that there were scarcely any white radicals who understood the importance of this. Those who did were mainly students whose politics led them towards uncritical adulation of the black movement and away from trying to build amongst white workers.

The ultimate tragedy was that the League had fallen apart by 1973, a year which witnessed an upsurge in wildcat strikes with thousands of black and white workers fighting side by side.

Another direction—cultural nationalism

WHILE THOSE such as the Panthers and DRUM at least attempted to find a strategy which could successfully challenge the system as a whole, others ended up pursuing struggles which represented little or no threat at all to the state. The path of 'cultural nationalism' originated in the civil rights movement, but ended far from its traditions and aspirations.

The politics of cultural nationalism found expression in the struggle to win black studies programmes in the US education system. In the 1960s this demand often met with bitter resistance and produced enormous struggles in colleges like San Fransisco State University in California and occupations at places like

Northwestern University in Chicago. The culmination of the fight took place at the top colleges Cornell and Harvard. At one stage the successful Cornell fight involved armed students marching to demand a black studies programme. The history of black people and of the fight against racism had been written out of university courses ever since they were established.

It is a mark of the level of racism in the United States today that these black studies programmes are still under attack and have been a major target in George Bush's offensive against 'political correctness'. The emphasis on rediscovering the role of blacks in history, not only as victims, but as fighters, was and is to be absolutely welcomed. But for large parts of the movement the emphasis on culture came to be the goal of the movement itself and a substitute for practical struggle. Malcolm had called on people to 'go back to Africa in your minds' but to stay and fight in the US. The celebration of African culture, dress and food, came to be seen as liberation itself for the cultural nationalists.

One of the foremost cultural nationalists was Maulana Ron Karenga, who was typical in rejecting political struggle. He believed, 'We must free ourselves culturally before we free ourselves politically'. His organisation opposed the attempts of the Panthers to organise in California. Nor was the 'culture' he looked to one of blacks resisting racism. Rather, he upheld the most reactionary aspects of village life in Africa:

> What makes woman appealing is femininity but she can't be feminine without being submissive. The role of woman is to inspire her man, educate her children and participate in social development.
> Equality is false, it is the devil's concept. Our concept is complementary. Complementary means you complete or make perfect that which is imperfect. The man has any right that does not destroy the collective needs of his family.[13]

Huey Newton attacked the cultural nationalists' do-nothing position, calling them 'pork chop' nationalists with their emphasis on lifestyle which could easily be accommodated by society.

Cultural nationalism provided a way out of engaging in struggle, especially when the black movement declined in the 1970s. This was particularly true in the colleges. Here Afrocentrism became less a critique of right wing racist political theories and more an attack on the left, particularly Marxism.

There was however a much more compelling dead end for the movement than cultural nationalism, the lure of electoralism. Electoral politics has been the major form of black politics over the last 20 years. By its very nature it represents a sharp break with the militant struggle of the 1960s. However, its roots can be discerned among the conflicting strands of the Black Power movement. It has been an unmitigated disaster from the standpoint of the mass of black Americans.

Crisis to fall:
Black Power as electoral power

THE CRISIS for the left of the black movement created a vacuum for other forces to step into. As we have seen, the ruling class was ready to grasp this breathing space in order to stabilise the situation by developing a black middle class, with black elected office holders as intermediaries between it and the mass of the black population. We have also seen that there were middle class black forces on hand, ready to step into such a role.

This phase, most crucially the move to electing black officials, frames the situation for blacks in the US today.

The black movement's 1972 Gary Convention marked the effective end of the great unrest of the 1960s and the replacement of mass mobilisation with electoral activity. While different tendencies were represented, the more conservative elements dominated it. The confusion among radicals about electoralism left them in no position to stop the stampede rightwards and the slogan of black unity came more explicitly to tie black workers and radicals to the middle class. Black elected officials could claim to represent the interests of all blacks, yet the record of black elected officials, overwhelmingly members of the Democratic Party, is appalling.

The first black mayor to be elected in any major US city was Carl Stokes in Cleveland in November 1967. He had attacked racism and police brutality during the campaign, which helped him to mobilise a record black vote and win 95 percent of it. One of his first decisions on becoming mayor was to appoint Benjamin O Davis, a former black general, as director of public safety. Davis sided completely with the police and he was more concerned with repressing radical black nationalists than in pursuing white racists who attacked black neighbourhoods. He even backed a police call for 'dum-dum' bullets.

Stokes was faced with racist opposition but there was a much more obvious problem. Cleveland, like most major cities, was sinking into financial crisis. There was scarcely any scope for satisfying the huge expectations of blacks and those whites who voted for him (one fifth of the vote). He made cut backs and sat out a sanitation strike and a transit strike in 1970. When Cleveland threatened to burst into riot as it had done in 1966, Stokes sent black police officers to the Hough area to make arrests.

The experience of Stokes in Cleveland set the pattern for a number of cities with black mayors in the 1980s. The disillusionment amongst Cleveland's blacks was massive. Black voter turnout in general elections plummeted from 81.7 percent in 1967 to 47.7 percent in 1979.

As economic crisis ravaged the US in 1974 and at both the beginning and end of the 1980s, the administration of every city went on the offensive against the municipal workforce, cut back on welfare, and generally defended the interests of the rich and privileged. Whether it was black or white administrations which presided over this made precious little difference. Nor could the increased number of blacks in the US Congress do anything to ameliorate the national attacks on welfare provision.

The hope that black elected officials, even if unable to do anything in material terms to help the poor, would at least be more liberal, was proved to be misplaced. The most notorious incident took place in Philadelphia.

Black radicals had faced systematic repression in Philadelphia since a raid on the SNCC headquarters in 1966 in which the police claimed to have discovered dynamite. The deputy police commissioner at the time was Frank Rizzo, a notoriously thuggish racist who was elected mayor in 1971.

One of the major reasons why so many blacks voted the city's first black mayor, W Wilson Goode, into office in 1985 was the hope that he would do something to curtail the cops' brutality. Instead, he carefully planned to launch an assault on the 'MOVE' black counter-cultural organisation which occupied a well defended building in West Philadelphia. On 12 May 1985, Goode ordered the police to drop a bomb into the building. As it exploded, a ball of fire, 4,000°C hot, caused nearby buildings to erupt into flames. Only two out of 13 men, women and children survived the firebomb and the lines of rifle fire the police laid across the rear of the house.

The social divide

WHEN THE movement was over and the dust settled it was possible to see who had benefitted from the tumultuous struggles of the 1960s. In the early 1970s,

> the upper fraction of the black labour force experienced a real advance in its absolute incomes. Between 1964 and 1974, for example, the earnings of the top 5 percent of all non-white families increased from $17,238 to $24,267; about 74 percent of the level for white families of a similar background. By 1977, 21 percent of all black families had incomes between $15,000 and $24,999, and another 9 percent earned over $25,000. Advances in income were more likely for those black families whose major 'breadwinner' had a college education... For... black husband-wife families below the age of 35 who were both income earners, the income gap between themselves and other white families with a similar socio-cultural profile virtually disappeared... The traditional income margin of racial inequality, at least for many of the black elite had been almost eliminated by the mid 1970s...[14]

> In 1977 ... the overall black unemployment rate for civilian workers was 13.1 percent for men, 14.8 percent for women. Black professional and technical workers, however, experienced unemployment rates of 6.1 percent for males, 5.1 percent for females.[15]

The affirmative action programmes, limited though they were, had clearly benefitted this layer of blacks. The new black professional classes totalled seven to 10 percent of the black population.

The integration of the black elite did not extend to the level of big business and the ruling class. In 1977 only 113 black owned businesses out of 231,195 had more than 100 employees, and another 230 had 50 to 99.

Even today the number of major black businessmen is insignificant. Rather, there was the development of an upwardly mobile professional middle class, with a number of small entrepreneurs. Their advances stood in contrast to the static or declining living standards of most blacks. Manning Marable has written:

> Now, in the post civil rights era of the 1980s and 1990s, even the definition of the 'black community' is up for debate. The net result of affirmative action and civil rights initiatives was to expand the potential base for the Afro-American middle class, which was located primarily outside the neighbourhood confines of the old ghetto. By 1989, one in seven African-American families had incomes exceeding $50,000 annually, compared to less than $22,000 for the average black household. Black college educated married couples currently earn 93 percent of the family income of comparable white couples.[16]

The growth in the number of elected black officials paralleled the growth of the black middle class. In 1966 there were less than 100 elected black officials in the US. In March 1969 there were 1,125, tripling to 3,499 by May 1975, with 18 blacks in Congress, 281 state legislators and 135 mayors. The figure now stands at something over 7,000. It is a cruel irony that now, with more blacks in positions of power than ever before, the majority of blacks are no better off than they were in 1965.

The rise of racism in the 1980s

AS THE number of black officials grew, the government rolled back many of the gains that had been won in the 1960s. In 1978 the Bakke decision in the Supreme Court set a precedent in deciding that affirmative action programmes constituted 'reverse racism'. The then president, Democrat Jimmy Carter, had been backed by the mainstream civil rights organisations. It was also under Carter that funding for abortion was outlawed and the tax burden started to shift from rich to poor.

Reagan took over from Carter and extended the attacks on welfare provision. The relative impoverishment of black workers was even more severe than that of white workers. In 1975 the median income of blacks was 63 percent that of whites, by 1991 the figure was 56 percent. Following in the footsteps of Nixon, Reagan's war on drugs and crime contained scarcely veiled racism. Theories about black criminality and deviance abounded.

In 1988 George Bush's election campaign featured racist propaganda about 'black crime'. He used the case of a convicted black rapist, Willie Horton, as a symbol of his readiness to crack down on blacks. He played openly to racist feelings.

The result of all this has been an increase in racist attacks all over the country. In 1986 Michael Griffiths was murdered by racists in Howard Beach, New York. Three years later Yusuf Hawkins was killed simply for being where he 'didn't belong'— the Bensonhurst area of New York.

The beating of Rodney Glen King by the Los Angeles police department was video recorded and shown coast to coast on TV. Yet the police were found not guilty by the courts, the spark for the 1992 riots. Racist organisations took their cue from the police. In Florida the Ku Klux Klan announced it would 'join the battle against illegal drugs [and] become the eyes and ears of the police'. They promised to catch 'black drug dealers'.

In 1987 the national unemployment rate among young black men stood at 34 percent, in some cities it was as high as 50 percent. In 1990 the British magazine, the **Economist** reported:

> The numbers are grim. Blacks are over twice as likely as whites to be jobless. The median black family income is 56 percent of a white family's. Nearly a third of all blacks, as against 10 percent of whites, live below what is officially reckoned as the poverty level. A newborn black baby is twice as likely as a white baby to die before its first birthday. The 31 million or so blacks are 12 percent of America's population but supply nearly half its prison population. A black man is six times as likely as a white man to be murdered; homicide is the leading cause of death of young black men.[17]

The **New England Journal of Medicine** 1990 report 'Excess Mortality in Harlem' concluded: 'life expectancy for a black male born and living in Harlem is shorter than that of a male born in Bangladesh'.[18]

Black college enrolment fell by 100,000 between 1980 and 1986; there are now more blacks in prison than attending college.

The 1960s saw a steady improvement in the living standards

of black and white workers, the gap between the two narrowing. The improvement in black living standards came in no small part as a result of the uprisings. The last 15 years have seen a reversal of that process with both black and white working class living standards falling and the gap between the two increasing.

Two responses have been thrown up by this situation. One is to head back to the streets in an attempt to regenerate some of the traditions of the civil rights movement. The other, at its most depressing, is for a tiny number of blacks to move right inside the ruling class itself.

Political responses—the right

CYNICISM about the electoral process has grown enormously among ordinary blacks. An increasing number of black politicians don't even present themselves as a continuation of the civil rights struggle, albeit in electoral form. They have been termed the 'post black politicians'.

Douglas Wilder, the governor of Virginia, proudly declares that he never went on a civil rights demonstration in his life. His 1989 campaign highlighted his support for the death penalty and anti union laws. Supreme Court Justice Clarence Thomas is committed to attacking affirmative action legislation. In the course of the shift to the right, politicians like these have fallen back on a rhetoric of self reliance and black advancement of the kind associated with Booker T Washington.

The confirmation of Clarence Thomas to the Supreme Court is instructive. Scarcely a day went by when he was testifying to the Senate committee in which he didn't mention his own 'humble origins', the poverty and hard work of his father. He didn't emphasise the assistance he got from affirmative action policies in his own education. He talked about racism and even quoted Malcolm X, but for him there was no institutional barrier to black advancement. It was simply a question of some blacks being treated unfairly.

The message was that blacks can make it. The only thing holding them back was themselves. It was a continuation of the Reaganite arguments that the reason why disproportionate numbers of blacks lived in poverty was the existence of a dependency culture. Such ideas provided cover for a sustained assault on working class living standards and the immiserisation of large sections of blacks.

Malcolm's palest reflection—community control

REVEREND Al Sharpton is today one of the most prominent black politicians outside the mainstream. Shunned as an FBI informant by many black activists, he nevertheless came to the fore in organising marches over the racist killings in Howard Beach in 1986 and Bensonhurst in 1989. His programme for change goes back to an idea popularised in the late 1960s, that of community control. Community control was foreshadowed by Malcolm shortly after his break with the Nation of Islam when he gave a definition of black nationalism:

> The political philosophy of black nationalism means that the black man should control the politics and the politicians of his own community...
> The economic philosophy of black nationalism is pure and simple. It means only that we should control the economy of our community...
> The social philosophy of black nationalism only means that we have to get together and remove the evils, the vices, alcoholism, drug addiction, and other evils that are destroying the moral fibre of our community.[19]

The idea of community control was used by left and right in the 1960s—despite the vagueness of its meaning—because it had mass appeal among black workers, reflecting the total control white people had over every aspect of black people's lives. Employers, police, city politicians, even most small businessmen in the ghettoes were white.

But there was a contradiction right at the heart of the attempt to build community control: how could it be won? Almost by definition, it was an alternative to any national strategy of confronting the authorities, yet if real power was to be exercised by the community it was the city, state and federal authorities who stood in the way. Rapidly the conclusion was drawn that this obstacle could be overcome through the election of black officials and met the same fate as others following the electoral strategy.

Divide and rule

THE DECLINE in politics and organisation among black people has allowed the US ruling class to wield an ancient weapon— divide and rule. In the desperate conditions of the US inner cities the ruling class has encouraged different groups among the deprived to be thought of as slightly better off than the poorest and most desperate. In many areas this divisive image is foisted on Koreans. In areas of New York blacks have been encouraged to see Jews as their marginally priviledged competitors.

This situation has often deflected black anger from those really to blame for police violence and economic deprivation, creating ugly incidents which many of today's black leaders have either been ill-equipped to deal with, or have even led in a reactionary direction.

For example, in August 1991 the anger among blacks in the Crown Heights area of New York exploded. The spark came when a Hasidic Jew ran over two black children. Gavin Cato died after the Hasidic ambulance that arrived was instructed by police to take only the driver to hospital. Three nights of rioting ensued in which a rabbinical student, Yankel Rosenbaum, was stabbed. He was taken to the local community hospital where he was left for several hours without treatment. His lungs filled with blood and he died.

The local black population rioted against the Jewish com- munity and the media rejoiced at supposed evidence of a 'race riot'. But the real cause was police brutality, racism and cut backs. Blacks and Jews had to compete for resources during the 1980s as funding was cut. Tragically, the anger was directed not against the real enemy—the police and city authorities—but towards the most visible target, the local Jewish population.

There was, however, another dynamic to the rioting. It became most intense when the police entered the area. Many blacks openly expressed their hostility to black Mayor David Dinkins when he visited the scene. Two days after, in East Flatbush, blacks fought back against a routine case of police victimisation. In other words, although misdirected, it was possible for the struggle to be turned against the racists and not against Jews. To do that would mean fighting anti semitic outbursts and building a struggle against those who really do oppress blacks in New York. Such a movement would necessarily have to confront the city's black mayor and would have to appeal to workers across New York who had the power to wring extra funds from the government.

But black leaders who intervened in Crown Heights—especially Al Sharpton—consciously stoked up anti semitism. Sharpton deliberately organised a march on a Saturday, the Jewish Sabbath. Its original destination was to be the headquarters of the Lubavitcher Jews.

Such leadership can claim nothing in common with the tradition of Malcolm X and represents no threat to the strategy of the US ruling class: better blacks never riot or protest at all; if they do, better they attack the Jews than the police.

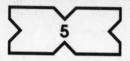

Socialism or black nationalism

THE IMPASSE in the struggle against racism in the US is all the more stark given the heights reached by the black movement in the 1960s.

The decline and eventual disintegration of the movement cannot be blamed on Malcolm who was killed in 1965. One aspect of his legacy is clear and in stark contrast to most of those who have followed: Malcolm was against any compromise with the system. He sought a revolutionary solution to end racism, understood this fight in a global context and was beginning to link the struggle against racism with the fight against capitalism:

> We are living in an era of revolution, and the revolt of the American Negro is part of the rebellion against the oppression and colonialism which has characterised this era...
> It is incorrect to classify the revolt of the Negro as simply a racial conflict of black against white, or as purely an American problem. Rather, we are today seeing a global struggle of the oppressed against the oppressor, the exploited against the exploiters.[1]

Nevertheless, the ambiguities and confusion in Malcolm's politics, and within black nationalism more generally, are important matters. We have seen how Black Power could be a slogan of the left or the right, how the idea of black unity came up against the growing class polarisation within the black population, how community control became a vehicle for careerist politicians or a dead end. Above all, we have witnessed the extraordinary lengths to which the US ruling class will go in order to preserve its power.

The black nationalist strategy has been tried and tested over three decades. It has failed. It remains, therefore, for us to find the power that can beat racism, and the politics to organise it.

Let us start by looking at the relationship between racism, capitalism and the working class.

White workers—a stake in the system?

THE UNDERLYING assumption of black nationalism is that all whites are racist or at least have a stake in the system. This is equally true, argue the nationalists, of white bosses and white workers. Even Malcolm, who believed it was possible to forge alliances with some 'sincere whites', did not look to white workers as members of the working class but rather to white 'militants'. In the mid 1960s this referred mainly to students.

What is at issue is not whether many white workers hold racist ideas, that is obviously so. The question is whether it is in their interests to do so and therefore whether they will always hold to racism.

Racism has been repeatedly used by the bosses as a tool in the class struggle. But why would the bosses use racism if it led to gains for white workers, who are the vast majority of the working class in the Western countries? For the bosses, their whole aim in the class struggle is to concede as little as possible to the working class. In fact, racism is used by the bosses to weaken the position of *all* workers. As one writer has pointed out:

> The existence of a segregated black workforce with inferior status limited, rather than enhanced, the ability of white workers to improve their wages and working conditions. In fact, employers were often willing to use, or threaten to use, black workers as strikebreakers or simply replacements, to keep white workers in line... [otherwise] it would be difficult to understand why employers followed racist hiring patterns if it enhanced the power of the overwhelming majority of the working class.[2]

All the evidence points to the fact that white workers have an objective, material interest in *ending* the oppression of blacks as their own living standards are held back by such racist divisions. One study which compared wage rates of black and white workers in the North and South of the US concluded that in the South, where racism was deeper and unionisation and working class solidarity correspondingly weaker, not only were black wages for the job lower but so too were the wages of whites. According to one author:

> what is most dramatic—in each of these blue collar groups, the southern white workers earned less than northern black workers. Despite the continued gross discrimination against black skilled craftsmen in the North, the 'privileged' southern whites earned 4 percent less than they did. Southern male white operatives averaged... 18 percent less than northern black male operatives. And Southern white service workers earned ... 14 percent less than northern black male service workers.[3]

Such findings can only make sense if racism is understood as an ideology that serves the interests of the ruling class rather than some conspiracy of all whites. Sociologist Al Syzmanski compared black and white earnings and discovered:

1. The higher black earnings relative to white, the higher white earnings relative to other whites.
2. The greater the discrimination against Third World people [mainly blacks, but also Hispanics], the higher the inequality among whites.[4]

He also found that, among whites, it is the poorest who lose out most from discrimination.

The working class and racism

IF IT IS not in the interests of the working class to accept racist ideas, why do so many workers continue to do so?

Part of the answer is straight forward. We are surrounded by racist propaganda, from the education system through to the mass media and outbursts from politicians. The idea that racial differences are significant and imply superiority or inferiority is deeply embedded in capitalist society. Overtly racist language may be less respectable now than in the 1960s, yet racist allusions to 'cultural differences' are invoked constantly. Racist undercurrents run through government pronouncements on drugs and law and order. Racism is part of every immigration control and attack on 'foreigners' wrecking 'our' country.

However, this is only part of the answer. Racism can lodge in the minds of workers because it appears to correspond to *one part* of their experience of living under capitalism—the compulsion to compete in order to get by. As Karl Marx explained, competition invades all aspects of society, and 'separates individuals from one another, not only the bourgeois but still more the workers'.[5]

Competition sets people apart from one another. We are encouraged to see the world through individual eyes. For the white worker living on a run down housing estate, feeling there is no possibility of change through collective struggle, it can seem the solution is to take housing from black people. Racism can appear to make sense.

Racism, however, only appears to make sense in the context of *one part* of the white worker's experience under capitalism. For, much as the bosses may loath the fact, they also have to bring workers together in order to organise production.

As we have seen, black workers who came to the cities of the US during this century were forced to live apart from whites. Nevertheless, even in the US, black and white workers are placed literally side by side in the workplaces. Workers therefore have a common experience of exploitation at the hands of the bosses. This fact lays the basis for the possibility of workers—black and white—feeling themselves to be part of a group which has collective interests and the ability to fight for them.

The more workers succeed in uniting and fighting, the less relevant seem the individualism and ideas of competition which stoke racism. This is why workers have the potential to radically transform society. They may hold rotten ideas at a given time, but they also have the potential to discard them.

On the face of it, prospects for working class unity can seem to be caught in a Catch 22. White workers can only overcome racism by uniting with their black brothers and sisters in a common struggle; yet racism is a powerful obstacle to their uniting in the first place. Moreover the process by which racist ideas are challenged and rejected on a mass level is by no means automatic. This has led some activists into seeing no basis for working class unity at all and to caricature socialists as wanting to 'wait until the revolution'.

In fact socialists argue for a fight against racism at all times, just as we always argue for a fight against the bosses. Success in one can feed success in the other. We also realise that the outcome of struggles can be crucially affected by the balance of argument in the struggle between right and left; between racists and anti racists.

The working class and anti racism

THE SECOND problem with the argument that all whites are racist is that it stands at odds with the history of the working class. Whilst many workers did and do accept racist ideas, there is also a long and deep *anti* racist tradition.

Anti racism has enjoyed only minority support during times of deep political reaction. But at times of increased working class confidence it has been able to challenge the dominant racist ideology. This is no new phenomenon.

The most prominent leaders of the first working class movement, the Chartists in Britain, were Bronterre O'Brien, Feargus O'Connor and William Cuffay. Cuffay was black, the other two Irish. This was at a time when racism against Irish and black people was a central ideological prop for British imperialism. Cuffay was so identified with the movement, which was overwhelmingly white in composition, that the **Times**, in an effort to belittle the Chartists, referred to them as 'that black man and his party'.[6]

Robert Wedderburn, a black man, was a key leader of an earlier movement, the Radicals. He was a very popular speaker and could draw an audience of hundreds of white workers from the East End of London. In 1819, shortly before he was imprisoned, he spoke to a packed meeting on the subject of slavery:

> Wedderburn, who described himself as *'The Offspring of an African'*, was *'highly gratified'* by the outcome of a debate on whether a slave had the right to kill a master. The question 'was decided in favour of the slave without a dissenting voice, by a numerous and enlightened assembly, who exultingly expressed their desire of hearing of another sable nation freeing itself by the dagger from the base tyranny of their Christian masters'; indeed, *'several gentlemen declared their readiness to assist them'*.[7]

The British ruling class backed the slave holding South in the American Civil War. The prime minister, Palmerstone, attempted to build popular support for the Southern cause and organised a number of public rallies. The cotton mills of Lancashire were heavily dependant on cotton produced by slave labour, as were the docks at Liverpool, and the blockade of southern ports had led to lay offs in both these areas. The British ruling class hoped to rally the poor and unemployed under the racist banner. When they attempted to hold a meeting in Liverpool, however, the speakers were chased away and a huge crowd of workers pledged support for the Northern forces and the abolition of slavery.

In America both before and during the Civil War large numbers of whites joined the militant abolitionist camp. They criticised Abraham Lincoln for not making the abolition of slavery the aim of the war with the South. The most famous of these was John Brown, who attempted to initiate a slave revolt by leading a group of black and white opponents to slavery in armed attacks on slave owners. Leading black abolitionist Frederick Douglass paid tribute to him:

> If John Brown did not end the war that ended slavery, he did, at least, begin the war that ended slavery. If we look over the dates, places and men for which this honour is claimed, we shall find that not Carolina, but Virginia, not Fort Sumter, but Harper's Ferry, and the arsenal, not Major Anderson, but John Brown began the war that ended American slavery, and made this a free republic. Until this blow was struck, the prospect for Freedom was dim, shadowy and uncertain.[8]

During what was known as reconstruction in the South between 1867 and 1877 an effective alliance was formed between poor white farmers and newly freed black slaves. The defeat of reconstruction gave birth to Jim Crow and a resurgence of racism. The Populists in the 1890s for a time united blacks and whites. It was only with the movement's defeat that many of the whites involved in it succumbed to racism.

When these struggles advanced, racism could be challenged on a mass scale. Poor whites began to identify with blacks rather than with the ruling class. The consciousness of white workers was not instantly transformed, but as people struggled against the rich and powerful, and ceased to act in a 'normal', passive way, then so too the normal common sense no longer fitted as an adequate explanation of society.

There was no inevitability in these struggles rooting out racism, but nor was it inevitable that the spontaneous black and white unity they achieved would be ruptured by the racism of the bosses. This depended on the level of solidarity that had been forged and on the fights between racists and anti racists.

Far from the ruling class simply offering racist ideas to a receptive working class, they constantly had to fight to shore up racism. That fight involved not only suppressing blacks but defeating white workers as well.

Those who argue against the possibility of uniting black and white workers point to the grimmest periods of working class history—when competition rather than solidarity were to the fore—in order to support their position. Let's now look at some of the reasons why racism has often had the upper hand against anti racism.

Black workers and the unions

ONE OF THE major factors at the beginning of this century that led many American blacks to believe they could not look to white workers for solidarity was the racism to be found in the trade unions. The American Federation of Labour held the affiliation of most of the major unions. It had supplanted an earlier and much better tradition. The Knights of Labour organised all grades of workers and had 60,000 black members at its height in 1886. The majority of the AFL unions either refused to organise Blacks or did so in segregated locals (branches). Ironically, Samuel Gompers, the leader of the AFL, who in the 1910s defended this policy, had two decades before taken a solidly anti racist position.

Gompers and the AFL had degenerated not simply because they collapsed into racism. More significantly, the AFL became an organisation which excluded most workers—white as well as black. It organised only a narrow band of skilled workers which necessarily meant it didn't organise blacks. It also meant that it didn't organise the majority of white workers who were unskilled.

These unions had a conservative outlook, more concerned to enter a 'partnership with business' than to lead a fight to defend workers' interests. This narrow 'craft' unionism fused with all sorts of elitist ideas, including of course racism. In other words, the adaptation of the unions to racism has to be understood as part of a wider political weakness. In turn, the fact that those white workers who were in unions weren't organised alongside blacks meant that united action was more difficult to achieve. It meant there was little counterweight to the bosses' racist propaganda.

The AFL tradition did not go unchallenged. The 'Wobblies', the Industrial Workers of the World (IWW), was established as an alternative to the AFL in 1905. It ran repeated campaigns to win black workers and never organised a segregated union, even when the law insisted on it. One estimate is that a tenth of the IWW's one million members recruited between 1909 and 1924 were black.

The AFL was also challenged with the emergence of the Congress of Industrial Organisations in the mid 1930s which organised among the growing numbers of unskilled workers. New general unions were built which organised blacks as well as whites in the centres of US capitalism, in autos, steel and engineering. The Congress passed this excellent resolution:

> *Whereas*, Employers constantly seek to split one group of workers from another, and thus to deprive them of their full economic strength by arousing prejudices based on race, creed, color or nationality, and one of the most frequent weapons used by employers to accomplish this end is to create false contests between Negro and white workers, now therefore be it
> *Resolved*, that the CIO hereby pledges itself to uncompromising opposition to any form of discrimination, whether political or economic, based on race, color, creed or nationality.[9]

The twin legacy of the Communist Party.

ONE OF THE factors that led militants towards black nationalism in the 1960s was the near-absence of a socialist alternative. This has not always been the case in the past and need not be in the future. The US socialist tradition is particularly weak for a number of specific reasons.

The Communist Party made efforts to organise among blacks throughout the 1920s. Initially, like most other socialists, they had taken an abstract position to the question of racism. They were opposed to racism but did not see it as something which had to be specifically fought. They saw it as something which would be overcome in the course of the class struggle. However, after significant pressure from Lenin and other Russian revolutionaries they started to make efforts to specifically organise blacks and to take up campaigns against racism, whether they were based in the workplaces or not. They attracted a small number of black radicals in the early 1920s when they were joined by Cyril Briggs and other leaders of the African Black Brotherhood. The ABB was a radical black nationalist organisation founded in the 'Red Summer' of 1919. The breakthrough for the Communist Party came in the early 1930s.

In 1931 they launched a campaign to defend the Scottsboro Boys—nine young black men who had been framed for the rape of two white women and who faced the death sentence. The CP built up impressive support in Harlem through tirelessly taking up the issue and refusing to follow the narrow legalistic approach of the NAACP which opposed demonstrations and protests over the case. They began to recruit significant numbers of blacks, with 700 members in Harlem by 1936. They also organised hundreds of black and white sharecroppers in Alabama. They did so because they refused to compromise with racism and because they didn't modify their radicalism to attract 'respectable opinion'.

It is often argued that the CP betrayed the black struggle after reaching an influential position. This is partly true, but the failure of the CP to lead a fight for black liberation is inseparable from its own abandonment of revolutionary socialism.

Like the Communist Parties everywhere, the American CP became a tool of Russia's foreign policy with the triumph of Stalin's counter revolution. Stalin's Popular Front policy in the 1930s meant the US party began to argue for an 'American', non violent path to socialism. In 1938 activists were told not to struggle against 'progressive officials' like President Roosevelt.

They supported the 'socialist' USSR when it supplied oil to

Mussolini during his invasion of Abyssinia and slavishly defended the Hitler-Stalin pact in 1939. Hundreds of blacks left the party. The Second World War brought renewed struggle in the factories and the demand from blacks that if they were being drafted to 'fight the fascist menace' then they should not have to face racism from the American state and fight in segregated units. Philip A Randolph organised a march on Washington to protest against this in 1943 (the march was later called off). The CP—loyal to the Russian ruling class then allied to the US bosses, rather than to the American working class—denounced the idea of the march, calling Randolph a 'scab'.

The pre war experience of the 1930s shows that white workers can be won over to the fight against racism. The eventual failure of the CP over tackling racism is not an argument for the irrelevance of socialism. It is an indication of their own departure from the genuine socialist tradition and is inseparable from it.

Black nationalism—a defensive reaction

WHEN THE US working class was on the offensive in the mid 1930s black nationalist ideas and organisations became marginalised. The potential to build a united fight and transform society could be proved in practice.

The great periods of growth in black nationalist organisation were during the 1920s and 1960s. Certain common factors gave rise to both. There were rising expectations among blacks in the wake of the First World War and the long boom respectively. There was also a racist backlash. Above all, although there was some wider radicalisation in society, there were no sustained struggles by white workers which brought them into confrontation with the state and with their own racist prejudices.

The black movement of the 1960s was distinguished by its identification with revolution. This revolutionary character came not from black nationalism, but from the militancy of the mass of blacks.

Malcolm had to constantly reassess his own black nationalist assumptions. He abandoned the separatism of the Nation of Islam and placed himself squarely against the system. He recognised that capitalism could not advance the majority of blacks. In taking such an uncompromising stance he, along with the black revolutionaries who followed him, was faced with the question of how to win. If black nationalism is a defensive reaction which grows in response to rising racism and the absence of a united fight against it, how can we take the offensive against racism?

Unity today

IF WE look below the surface then we can see that there is the possibility of black and white workers fighting together. In Britain there is a very good recent experience of such struggles, from the solidarity shown around the Grunwicks strike in West London, to action over the sacking of a black shop steward in the Longbridge car plant, to black and white workers standing shoulder to shoulder on transport, hospital, local government and Ford picket lines.

The experience of united action in the US might seem less obvious, as black and white people still live largely separately in most big cities. However, every major strike—in the car plants, the post office, the hospitals in New York in 1990 or at Caterpillar in 1991—involves black workers as well as white.

Moreover, black and white have fought alongside each other in the place where there are fewer pressures towards unity—in the streets. Almost all recent riots in Britain have involved both black and white people. More dramatically, the riots which spread from Los Angeles in the spring of 1992 involved white people fighting alongside blacks against police brutality, a completely different situation from the all-black riots of the 1960s. The riot, with 54 dead, 4,000 arrested and only quelled with the assistance of 4,000 troops and 6,000 National Guards was on the same scale as the 1964 Watts rising. This time, however, an estimated 30 percent of the rioters were white. This fact, plus the many demonstrations involving both black and white people across the country, dealt an enormous blow to racism.

As the crisis of capitalism continues, then bosses try to make racism a tool to break up such solidarity. For white workers therefore the question of overcoming racism is a matter of direct and material interest. They will be thrown into experiences of struggle in which they will have to challenge racism in order to preserve solidarity.

There is no doubt these struggles will come. The question is whether activists are in a position to lead a fight against racism and for solidarity, or whether the field is cleared for the bosses' arguments to take hold.

The means necessary

THE STRATEGY of revolutionary socialism has always been to build the maximum unity in the working class in the fight against racism. This has meant not only opposing racism in principle but presenting arguments in class terms to white workers which explain their own interest in fighting racism. There are two things to be said about the nature of the united response socialists seek to build.

First, it is not based on the abstract notion that socialism is 'colour blind'. Racism is used *actively* by the bosses and their media and therefore needs to be fought actively. The argument for unity in the working class is not designed to submerge the fight against oppression but to bring it to the fore and make it central to the fight against capitalism.

Secondly, while large scale struggles by workers can create the conditions for undermining racism on a mass scale, socialists do not passively wait for this to happen. Even in the most unfavourable circumstances the systematic fight to win white workers away from racist ideas and involve them alongside blacks in anti racist activity continues. Unity has to be fought for and demonstrated in practice. Even when workers spontaneously overcome racism to unite, this unity has to be generalised. Workers who learn that racism makes no sense in their own workplace or community must be encouraged to take up wider questions of racism, like police brutality or immigration controls.

Above all, the revolutionary socialist position on fighting racism is based on an uncompromising opposition to the system that breeds it. Malcolm had grasped the fact that capitalism and racism were intertwined declaring: 'You can't have capitalism without racism.'[10]

The British Labour Party is a prime illustration of the

difficulties faced in fighting racism by those who accommodate to capitalism. The party contains many committed anti racists, but Labour's whole strategy is based on winning reforms within capitalism. This has always meant preserving capitalism. In times of economic crisis this means making workers pay for that crisis through wage cuts and layoffs. It means presiding over the very conditions in which racist ideas can flourish.

On top of that, the Labour Party is an electoralist party. It seeks 'power' through winning votes. It relates to workers when they are most passive, as isolated individuals, not as a collective force. In its desire to win elections it adapts to the lowest common denominator. If racist ideas are growing in society, the Labour Party will adapt to them. Of course it will continue to denounce racism, but in practice it behaves no differently to the Tory Party when it comes to the things that shape black workers' lives. In government the Labour Party has repeatedly tightened immigration controls.

These horrible aspects of the Labour tradition, of reformism, are not an indictment of the genuine socialist tradition. They are not part of the tradition of struggle from below. It is Labour's insistence on change from above that leads it to adapt to racism. It hasn't grasped the simple truth summed up by black abolitionist Frederick Douglass: 'without struggle there can be no progress'.

Revolutionary socialists, on the other hand, argue for struggle, both to change society and to change workers themselves. As Karl Marx said:

> the revolution is necessary, therefore, not only because the ruling class cannot be overthrown in any other way, but also because the class overthrowing it can only in a revolution succeed in ridding itself of all the old crap and become fitted to found society anew.[11]

Socialists, the working class and the oppressed

SOCIALISTS argue for a different kind of party to that of Labour. Instead of being passive and embarrassed in the face of oppression, socialists should be the 'tribunes of the people', as Lenin said, able to, react to every manifestation of tyranny and oppression, no matter where it takes place, no matter what stratum or class of people it affects; ... able to generalise all these manifestations to produce a single picture of police violence and capitalist exploitation; ... able to take advantage of every event, however small, in order to explain his socialist convictions and his democratic demands to all, in order to explain to all and everyone the world historic significance of the proletariat's struggle for emancipation.[12]

In other words revolutionaries had to take up the fight against oppression at every stage. Lenin went on to say that socialists should support struggles by the oppressed even when led by anti socialists. What was important was the fact that people fought back. As long as people were fighting the system, even if not inspired by socialist ideas, then they would weaken the capitalist system even if it took a revolutionary movement of the working class to overthrow it.

Additionally, when people fight they have to consider the best strategies and politics for the struggle. Not everyone leaves the battlefield with the same ideas they started with. Some stay committed to a set of ideas which could only advance the movement to a certain stage at a certain time, others are compelled to look to increasingly radical solutions.

This process affected Malcolm. There has been much debate about whether he was on the verge of becoming a revolutionary socialist when he was assassinated. It is impossible to predict the exact evolution of Malcolm's politics. He could have gone in a number of directions. Speculation obscures the central importance of Malcolm's last year. He moved enormously from his previously held beliefs. Moreover, he unambiguously moved to the left in the last months of his life. He became an uncompromising revolutionary. This meant he had to progressively abandon all sorts of separatist and black nationalist ideas. The same process was at work with the Panthers and DRUM.

When workers took to the streets of Russia in 1917, demanding basic rights and the end of the monarchy they began a process which culminated in working class power in October. As people swung to the left there was an organisation which could provide a coherent framework for them and a deeper explanation of what was needed to be done. The Bolsheviks could guide the revolution through ups and downs and eventually lead the successful insurrection.

For those radicals who were politicised in the 1960s there was no organisation which could provide that anchorage. Those socialists that did exist in the main accepted that the black movement had to be autonomous, generating theories that black nationalism in the US was inherently revolutionary. As a result they were badly placed to offer a socialist alternative.

Lenin insisted not only upon unconditionally supporting the struggles of the oppressed but also upon the independence of socialists and showing in practice the superiority of socialist ideas and methods. This means a political struggle with black nationalist ideas at the same time as supporting and building the broader movement. Such an approach could have won the best sections of the movement in the 1960s. It could have pulled together the anti war movement with the black struggle. It could also have organised that minority of white workers who did want to change the system.

This approach needs to be taken today. To pick up where Malcolm left off we need to understand developments since his death and the relevance of the classical Marxist tradition which Malcolm remained ignorant of during his too brief life.

The conditions which created the rebellion of the 1960s are still in place. There is every reason to expect outbursts of anger in the future as US society becomes more polarised and continues to stagger from crisis to crisis. When those struggles do take place they will be the result of accumulated bitterness at racism, recession, cut backs and unemployment. In the major cities people will not be up against all-white establishments, but—as during the 1992 Los Angeles riots, which took place in a city with a black mayor—ones which to varying degrees have a significant black middle class component.

The numbers of blacks who have a stake in the system is tiny, although their social weight is much greater. This, however, cuts both ways. The elevation to office of black mayors and police chiefs wrong-footed the movement in the 1970s. Now, however, their existence can weaken the notion that all blacks should stand together against 'white society'. On the contrary, in the early 1990s, class was reasserting itself as the key divide in society.

Black workers will have to confront that layer of middle class blacks who have made their peace with the system. That is not to say that black nationalist ideas will not play a role, but they will face contradictions much more stark than those in the 1960s.

By the same token, there is no reason to suppose that, given the savage attacks on US workers over the last decade, white workers will not be part of any fight back. Black workers will be central to such struggles. In 1922 the Communist International of revolutionary parties recognised:

> The history of the American blacks has prepared them to play a major role in the liberation struggle of the entire African race. Three hundred years ago the American blacks were torn from their native African soil, transported to America in slave ships and, in indescribably cruel conditions, sold into slavery... The Civil War, which was not a war for the emancipation of the blacks but a war for the preservation of the industrial capitalism of the North, confronted the blacks with a choice between forced labour in the South and wage slavery in the North... Black soldiers had hardly returned from the bloodbath of the [First World] war before they came up against racial persecution, lynchings, murder, the denial of rights, discrimination and general contempt. They fought back, but paid dearly for the attempt to assert their human rights... The spirit of revolt, inflamed by the post war violence and persecution, was suppressed, but cases of inhuman cruelty... still cause it to flare up again. This, plus the post war industrialisation of the blacks in the North, places the American blacks, particularly those in the North, in the vanguard of the struggle for black liberation.[13]

This fact makes the struggle in the United States of international importance. Malcolm understood that. His life is a testament to the brutality of racism and the courage and capacity of people to rise up and resist it. His uncompromising revolutionary spirit led him to move to the left to find answers to the questions which confronted him. He was cut down before he could find those answers. But the fact that he fought will ensure that for years to come he will be an inspiration to those involved in the same struggle.

The biggest tribute we can pay him is for those of us who share those goals of freedom, justice and an end to exploitation and oppression to fight by any means necessary. We must also learn the lessons of the past. We don't dismiss what has been achieved. We want to build on it, preserve what is useful and reject what is not—the better to win the next time.

Notes

Introduction

1. **New York Times**, 22 February 1965.
2. Manning Marable, **Race, Reform and Rebellion: The Second Reconstruction, 1945-1982**, London 1984, p. 101.
3. **New York Times**, 5 November 1965.
4. Truman Nelson, 'Delinquent's Progress', **The Nation**, 8 November 1965.
5. **Muhammed Speaks**, 10 November 1964.
6. Vladimir Lenin, **Collected Works**, vol. 25, translated from the fourth Russian edition, p. 385.
7. John Henrik Clarke, **Malcolm X, the Man and his Times**, New York 1969, p. 209.

Chapter 1. The world of Malcolm X

1. **The Autobiography of Malcolm X**, Harmondsworth 1985, p. 80.
2. Ibid., p. 81.
3. Leon Trotsky, **On Black Nationalism**, New York 1967, p. 46.
4. A Pinkney, **Red, Black and Green: Black Nationalism in the United States**, New York 1978, p. 48.
5. E David Cronon, **Black Moses: The Story of Marcus Garvey**, Wisconsin 1969, p. 190.
6. Ibid., p. 198.
7. Quoted in Ahmed Shawki, 'Black Liberation and Socialism in the United States', **International Socialism**, 2:47, London 1990, p. 77.

Chapter 2. The life of Malcolm X.

1. C Eric Lincoln, **The Black Muslims in America,** Boston 1961, p. 97.
2. Quoted in Ahmed Shawki, 'Black Liberation and Socialism in the United States', **International Socialism,** 2:47, London 1990, p. 79.
3. Louis E Lomax, **To Kill a Black Man,** Los Angeles 1968, p. 61.
4. J Bloom, **Class, Race and the Civil Rights Movement,** Indiana 1987, p. 194.
5. Howard Zinn, **SNCC,** Boston 1965, p. 234.
6. Quoted in ibid., p. 235.
7. Bloom, op cit., p. 194.
8. A Pinkney, **Red, Black and Green: Black Nationalism in the United States,** New York 1978, p. 67.
9. James Forman, **The Making of Black Revolutionaries,** Washington 1985, p. 317.
10. EV Wolferstein, **The Victims of Democracy: Malcolm X and the Black Revolution,** Berkeley 1981, p. 243.
11. Ibid., p. 271.
12. Ibid.
13. George Breitman, **The Last Year of Malcolm X,** New York 1967, p. 16.
14. George Breitman ed., **Malcolm X Speaks,** New York 1990, p. 201
15. Louis E Lomax, **When the Word is Given,** Cleveland 1963, p. 179.
16. Breitman, **The Last Year of Malcolm X,** p. 10.
17. Quoted in ibid., p. 20.
18. Lance Selfa, 'The Mississippi Freedom Summer', **Socialist Worker,** Chicago June 1989.
19. Ibid.
20. Breitman ed., op cit., pp. 201-2.
21. Manning Marable, **Race, Reform and Rebellion: The Second Reconstruction, 1945-1982,** London 1984, pp. 88-9.

Chapter 3. The thought of Malcolm X

1. George Breitman ed., **Malcolm X Speaks,** New York 1990, p. 20.
2. Ibid., p. 109-10.
3. Ibid., p. 133.
4. Ibid., p. 57.
5. George Breitman, **The Last Year of Malcolm X,** New York 1967, p. 23.
6. **The Autobiography of Malcolm X,** Harmondsworth 1985, p. 454.
7. Breitman ed., op cit., p. 38.

8. Quoted in ibid., pp. 64-5.
9. Quoted in ibid., p. 45.
10. Breitman, op cit., p. 46.
11. Breitman ed., op cit., pp. 206-7.
12. J Bloom, **Class, Race and the Civil Rights Movement**, Indiana 1987, p. 194.
13. EV Wolferstein, **The Victims of Democracy: Malcolm X and the Black Revolution**, Berkeley 1981, p. 12.
14. **Malcolm X On Afro American History**, New York 1990, p. 24-5.
15. Quoted in Breitman ed., op cit., p. 69
16. Ibid., p. 52.
17. Quoted in Clayborne Carson, **In Struggle: SNCC and the Black Awakening of the 1960s**, Cambridge Massachusetts 1981, p. 220.
18. Breitman, op cit., p. 46.
19. Breitman ed., op cit., pp. 68-9.

Chapter 4. The legacy of Malcolm X

1. John Henrik Clarke, **Malcolm X: The Man and his Times**, New York 1969, p. 209.
2. Joseph Boskin, **Urban Racial Violence**, Los Angeles 1969, p. 38.
3. Ibid., p. 126.
4. Manning Marable, **Race, Reform and Rebellion: The Second Reconstruction, 1945-1982**, London 1984, p. 104.
5. Ibid., pp. 105-6.
6. Stokeley Carmichael and C Hamilton, **Black Power**, New York 1970, p. 146.
7. Marable, op cit., p. 106.
8. Ibid., pp. 108-9.
9. James Forman, **The Making of Black Revolutionaries**, Washington 1985, p. 459.
10. Robert Allen, **Black Awakening in Capitalist America**, New York 1970, p. 47.
11. Bobby Seale, **Seize the Time**, London 1970, p. 473.
12. Quoted in James Geschwender, **Class, Race and Worker Insurgency**, Cambridge 1977, p. 138.
13. Allen, op cit., pp. 168-9.
14 Marable, op cit., 1991 edition, p. 151.
15. Ibid.
16. Quoted in Sharon Smith, 'Twilight of the American Dream', **International Socialism**, 2:54, London 1992, p. 20.
17. **Economist**, 3 March 1990.
18. **Washington Post**, 18 December 1990.

19. George Breitman ed., **Malcolm X Speaks**, New York 1990, pp. 38-9.

Chapter 5. Socialism or black nationalism

1. George Breitman ed., **Malcolm X Speaks**, New York 1990, p. 217.
2. M Glaberman, 'Class is a Missing Element', in **New Politics**, vol. 1 no. 3 (new series), New York 1987, p. 59.
3. Study cited in V Perlo, **Economics of Racism USA**, New York 1980, p. 168.
4. A Szymanski, 'Racial Discrimination and White Gain', in **American Sociological Review**, 41:3, 1976, pp. 409-10.
5. Quoted in Hal Draper, **Karl Marx's Theory of Revolution: The Politics of Social Classes**, New York 1978, p. 66.
6. Peter Fryer, **Staying Power: The History of Black People in Britain**, London 1984, p. 239.
7. Ibid., p. 223. Fryer's emphasis.
8. Quoted in B Quarles, **Frederick Douglass**, New York 1976, p 185.
9. P Foner, **Organised Labor and the Black Worker**, New York 1981, pp. 229-30.
10. Quoted in Breitman ed., op cit., New York 1981, p. 69.
11. Quoted in Draper, op cit., p. 74.
12. Vladimir Lenin, **What is to be Done?**, Beijing 1973, p. 104.
13. Quoted in David Widgery and Mike Rosen, **Voices of Dissent**, London 1991, p. 286.

Index

Abyssinia: 14, 81
Affirmative action: 43, 65-6, 68
Africa: 14, 35, 38, 44-5
African Blood Brotherhood: 80
Algeria: 33, 39, 47
Allen, Robert: 35, 55
American Federation of Labour (AFL): 13, 78-9
American Nazi Party: 32
American Revolution: 33
Anniston (Alabama): 26
Audubon Ballroom: 7
Autobiography of Malcolm X: 8, 11, 31
Azikwe, Nnamdi: 44

Baker, General: 59-60
Bakke decision: 66
Bensonhurst (New York): 67, 69
Birmingham (Alabama): 29
The Birth of a Nation: 12
Black Deacons of Defence: 52
Black middle class: 10, 18, 20-1, 29, 31, 43-4, 55-6, 63-6, 68-9, 86
Black Muslims: *see Nation of Islam*
Black nationalism (*see also Black Power, Cultural nationalism, Garvey, Nation of Islam etc.*): 13-14, 19-25, 35, 37-50, 52-6, 60, 61-3, 69-71, 72, 81-2, 85, 87
Black Panther Party for Self Defence: 46, 56-9, 61, 62, 85
Black Power: 47, 51-6, 72
Black separatism: *see Black nationalism*

Black Star Line: 14
Black studies: 61-2
Black voters: 22, 27, 36-8
Blair, Izell: 25
'Boynton vs Virginia': 26
Briggs, Cyril: 80
Britain: 41, 44, 46, 75-6, 82, 83-4
Brown, John: 77
'Brown vs Topeka Board of Education': 17
Bush, George: 62

California Peace and Freedom Party: 59
Carmichael, Stokely: 47, 52-3, 55
Carter, James: 66
Cato, Gavin: 70
Chaney, James: 34
Chartists: 76
Chrysler: 59-60
Civil rights legislation: 27, 29-30, 34
Civil rights movement:
—attacks on Malcolm X: 7-8
—beginnings: 16-18
—and Nation of Islam: 21-3
—and Democrats: 25-8
—non violence: 25
—mass movement: 25-6
—sit-ins: 25-6
—freedom rides: 26-7
—reined in by Kennedys: 27
—becomes radicalised, divisions emerge: 29-30, 33-5
—and Black Power: 52-4
Civil War: 12, 16, 77, 87

Communist International: 87
Communist Party: 22, 79-81
'Community control': 69
Congress of Industrial
Organisations: 22, 79
Congress of Racial Equality: 26-7,
29-30, 37, 52-4
Conservative Party (Britain): 44,
84
Crown Heights (New York): 9, 70-1
Cuffay, William: 76
Cultural nationalism: 61-3

Davis, Angela: 57
Davis, Benjamin O: 63-4
Declaration of Independence: 12
Democratic Party: 9, 17, 22, 27-8,
33-4, 36-8, 47, 52, 59, 63, 66
Desegregation: 17, 23, 26-7, 38
Detroit: 22, 52, 59-60
Dinkins, David: 9, 70
'Dixiecrats': 27
Dodge Revolutionary Union
Movement: 59-61, 85
Douglass, Frederick: 12, 77, 84
Drugs: 15, 67
Du Bois, WEB: 17, 21

Economic deprivation: 65-8
Eldon Avenue Revolutionary
Union Movement (ELRUM): 60-1
Electoralism: 63-5, 67, 68-9, 84
Emancipation: 23, 77
Evers, Medgar: 29

Fard, Wallace D: 19
Farmer, James: 26, 27
Farrakhan, Louis (Louis X): 9
Fascism, fascists: 14, 32
Federal Bureau of Investigation
(FBI): 34, 57, 69
First World War: 13, 15, 81, 87
Ford: 21, 59
Forman, James: 34, 55
French Revolution: 33

Garvey, M: 13-14, 20-1, 32
Gary Convention: 63
General Motors: 21, 59

Ghana: 39, 44, 47
Goldwater, Barry: 34
Gompers, Samuel: 78
Goode, W Wilson: 64-5
Goodman, Andrew: 34
Greensboro: 26
Griffiths, Michael: 67

Hamilton, Charles V: 53
Hammer, Fanny Lou: 36-7
Handler, MS: 33
Harlem: 7, 12, 13, 22, 51, 80
Hawkins, Yusuf: 67
Horton, Willie: 67
Howard Beach (New York): 67, 69

Industrial Workers of the World
('Wobblies'): 79
International Monetary Fund: 48
Iraq: 40, 48

Jackson, George: 57
Jackson, Jesse: 8-9
Jackson (Mississippi): 30
Jefferson, T: 12
Jim Crow: 12, 18, 22, 26, 29, 77
Johnson, Lyndon B: 27, 34, 37

Karenga, Maulana Ron: 62
Katzenbach, Nicholas: 34
Kennedy, John: 26-8, 29-30, 32-3
Kennedy, Robert: 27
Kenyata, Jomo: 44
King, Martin Luther: 8, 17-18, 22,
29-30, 32, 34-5, 52, 54
King, Rodney Glen: 67
Knights of Labour: 78
Ku Klux Klan: 12, 14, 16, 29, 32,
52, 67

Labour Party, Britain: 83-4
League of Black Revolutionary
Workers: 60
Lenin, Vladimir 9, 24, 47, 80, 84-6
Lewis, John: 26, 30
Liberia: 14
Lincoln, Abraham: 77
Little, Earl (Malcolm's father): 11,
12-13, 14

Little, Ella (Ella Collins, Malcolm's half sister): 15
Little, Louise (Malcolm's mother): 11, 14-15
Little Rock High School: 23
Lomax, Louis: 23
Los Angeles: 10, 22, 51, 67, 82, 86
Los Angeles Seven: 31

Malcolm X:
—killed: 7, 72
—transformation of ideas: 9
—born Malcolm Little: 11
—house firebombed: 11
—becomes a hustler: 15
—sent to jail: 16
—converts to Nation of Islam: 16
—steps to prominence: 18
—become National Minister: 19
—appears on TV: 23
—deals with 'reverse racism': 23-4, 28
—against non-violence: 28
—influences others: 30, 55, 56
—on March on Washington: 30
—frustrated at inactivity: 31-2
—warns Nazis: 32
—'chickens come home to roost': 32-3
—expelled from Nation of Islam: 33
—on Democratic Party, voting: 34, 36-7
—final year: 35, 36-50
—his thought: 36-50
—on role of whites: 38-42, 49
—goes to Mecca: 38
—founds Muslim Mosque Inc.: 39
—and socialists: 40, 45, 49
—on 'fed ups': 41
—on Black unity: 40-3
—'house Negroes and field Negroes': 43
—inspiration of Africa: 43-5
—on 'Negro', 'Afro-American', 'Black': 44-5
—on socialism: 45-6, 49-50
—'minorities and majorities': 46-8
—predicts riots: 51
—quoted by Clarence Thomas: 68
—defines black nationalism: 69
—for international revolution: 72
—forced to reconsider separatism: 85
—legacy today: 86-8
Mao Ze Dong: 58
Marable, Manning: 35, 66
March Against Fear: 52
March on Washington (1943): 81
March on Washington (1963): 29-30
Marx, Karl: 46, 75, 84
McCain, Franklin: 25
McKissick, Floyd: 52
McNeil, Joseph: 25
Mecca: 19, 38
Meredith, James: 26, 52
Mississippi Freedom Democratic Party: 37
Mississippi Summer Project: 33-4
Montgomery (Alabama): 17
MOVE: 65-6
Muhammad, Elijah (Elijah Poole): 19, 21, 28, 30-3
Muslim Mosque Inc.: 39, 40-1, 42
Mussolini, B: 14, 81

Nasser, Gamal Abdel: 44
Nation of Islam (Black Muslims): 9, 19-23, 25, 30, 31-3, 42, 49, 69, 81
National Association for the Advancement of Colored People (NAACP): 17, 22, 29, 52, 53, 80
Nationalism: 24
Newton, Huey: 56-7, 59, 62
Nixon, Richard: 27, 54-5, 57, 58, 67
Nkrumah, Kwame: 44
North Carolina Agricultural and Technical College: 25
Northwestern University: 62

Obote, Milton: 44
O'Brien, Bronterre: 76
O'Connor, Feargus: 76
Organisation of African Unity: 48
Organisation of Afro American Unity (OAAU): 41, 42

Parks, Rosa: 17
Philidelphia: 64-5
'Politically Correct': 62
Positive discrimination: *see
Affirmative action*
Powell, Adam Clayton: 53, 55

Race riots (1919): 13
Racism, general:
—general level of: 11-18, 66-8
—as ideology: 24, 73-9
—anti racism: 76-8, 82-8
Randolph, Philip A: 35, 81
Reagan, Ronald: 57, 66-7
Reconstruction: 12, 77
Republican Party: 9, 16, 22, 27, 59
'Reverse racism': 23-5, 28
Revolutionary socialism: 83-8
Richmond, David: 25
Rizzo, Frank: 64
Rockhill (South Carolina): 26
Rockwell, George Lincoln: 32
Roosevelt, President: 80
Rosenbaum, Yankel: 70
Rowan, Carl T: 7
Rubin, Jerry: 59
Russian Revolution: 85-6
Rustin, Bayard: 8, 47

San Fransisco State University: 61
Saudi Arabia: 39
Schwerner, Michael: 34
Scottsboro Boys: 80
Seale, Bobby: 56, 58
Second World War: 15, 16, 81
Self defence: 34, 56-9
Selma: 34-5
Sharpton, Rev. Al: 69, 71
Slavery: 11-12, 39, 87

Southern Christian Leadership
Conference (SCLC): 26, 53
Stokes, Carl: 63-4
Student Nonviolent Coordinating
Committee (SNCC): 26-7, 29-30,
33-5, 52-7, 64
Szymanski, Al: 74

Thomas, Clarence: 43, 68
Toure, Sekou: 44
Trotsky, Leon: 14, 47

Unemployment: 13, 15, 65, 67
United Auto Workers: 60
United Nations: 48
Universal Negro Improvement
Association (UNIA): 13-14
University of Mississippi: 26
Uprisings (1960s): 51-2

Vietnam War: 10, 27, 32, 34, 35,
47, 52, 54, 57

Wages, relative: 21, 67, 73-4
Washington, Booker T: 13, 20, 68
Watson, John: 60
Watts: *see Los Angeles*
Wedderburn, Robert: 76
Wilder, Douglas: 68
Wilkins, Roy: 35, 52
Working class: 41, 58, 59-61, 73-9,
82-7
—growth of black working class:
13, 15-16
World Bank: 48
Wright, Nathan: 54

Yacub: 19
Young, Andrew: 35

Bookmarks

265 Seven Sisters Road, London E3 3LH
PO Box 16085, Chicago, Il. 60616, US
GPO Box 1473N, Melbourne 3001, Australia